SUNDAY
by
SUNDAY

KEN TAYLOR

SUNDAY
by
SUNDAY

MEDITATIONS AND RESOURCES FOR
ALL APPOINTED GOSPEL READINGS
YEARS A, B AND C
REVISED COMMON LECTIONARY

VOLUME TWO
BETWEEN TRINITY AND ADVENT

Kevin Mayhew

First published in 2000 by
KEVIN MAYHEW LTD
Buxhall
Stowmarket
Suffolk IP14 3BW

0 1 2 3 4 5 6 7 8 9

ISBN 1 84003 490 4
Catalogue No 1500327

Cover design by Jaquetta Sergeant
Edited by Peter Dainty
Typesetting by Elisabeth Bates
Printed and bound in Great Britain

This book is dedicated
to the memory of

ERIC LEE THACKER
(1923-1997)

priest, pastor, preacher,
poet, artist, song-writer,
humorist, musicologist, jazz-pianist,
calligrapher and wordsmith

and my best friend and pal

ABOUT THE AUTHOR

Ken Taylor is a Methodist minister. Born in Hull and trained in Manchester, he has worked in Orrell, St Helens, Liverpool (Crosby), Leeds (Cross Gates) and Chester-le-Street. He is married, with four sons and a daughter. Retired early through ill-health, he now lives in Skipton, where he still conducts worship and preaches most Sundays. He is the author of *Praying the Passion*, meditations and prayers for Lent (Kevin Mayhew 1996), and *Cradle of Hope*, meditations for Advent and Christmas (Kevin Mayhew 1997). The first volume of *Sunday by Sunday* (Advent to Trinity) was published in 1999.

ACKNOWLEDGEMENTS

The *Revised English Bible* © Oxford University and Cambridge University Presses 1989, is used in all Scriptural quotations.

CONTENTS _____

YEAR B

YEAR C

FOREWORD

These meditations are intended both for devotional use and for resource purposes. They are based upon the Gospel reading appointed in the Revised Common Lectionary for each Sunday between Trinity and Advent.

The Lectionary focuses upon one of the first three gospels each year, in a three-year cycle. However, throughout the great seasons of Lent and Easter most of the readings are taken from John's gospel and it is only after Pentecost that the synoptic gospels come into their own.

For other Sundays from Advent to Trinity, the appointed Gospel each year is a parallel synoptic account of the same incident. In the first volume it seemed simplest to deal with all three narratives together, Sunday by Sunday.

The format of this book is different.

After Trinity Sunday, Matthew, Mark (with a complement from John), and Luke are used in successive years. The meditations in this book follow that order, in three separate sections.

Whether you use these meditations in your private prayers, or in Bible-study and discussion groups, or in sermon preparation, they are always best used alongside the relevant Bible passage.

KEN TAYLOR

THE NAMING OF SUNDAYS _____

It is quite exciting and good to know that at last on most Sundays the great majority of English-speaking Christians are reading and hearing the same passage from the Gospel.

However, there are still some variations in the names which the different denominations use to identify Sundays after Trinity to accommodate their own needs and preferences.

While the Revised Common Lectionary identifies Sundays after Trinity by the 'Proper' number, at the time of this book's publication, Methodists and Roman Catholics use 'Sundays in Ordinary Time', Anglicans identify 'Sundays after Trinity' and United Reformed Churches and the Church of Scotland use 'Sundays after Pentecost'.

This book follows the RCL naming, with the accompanying number in Ordinary Time.

However, calendar dates are also used in each case, which with the Gospel Index should make sure everyone can find their way around.

Please note:

In years when Trinity Sunday falls before May 28, the readings to be used are those appointed for Proper 3 (Epiphany 8). Meditations on those Gospel readings may be found in the first volume of *Sunday by Sunday*.

THE EAGLE AND THE OX,
THE WINGED MAN AND THE LION ──

The Gospels are not biographies, they are 'preaching'.

Traditionally compiled as a 'substitute for the living voice of the apostles', they were needed and used for worship, training, propaganda, guidance in Christian living, and defence against heresy and persecution.

But above all, they were written to bring the reader to a life-giving faith in Jesus Christ (see John 20:31).

However, each gospel-writer had his own clear characteristics and special interests, and his own theological viewpoint.

Each painted a picture of the Jesus he loved and followed.

The traditional symbols

St Jerome, the outstanding scholar of the early Church, was the first to suggest that the four evangelists should be symbolised by the 'four living creatures' of Revelation 4:6-8.

In the sixth century 'Book of Durrow', the first of the Celtic illuminated Gospels, an eagle is used to symbolise Mark, a man for Matthew, an ox for Luke, and a lion for John. In the more renowned Lindisfarne Gospels of the seventh century, Matthew has the symbol of the winged man, Mark the lion, Luke the ox, and John the eagle. This has become the accepted allocation of the symbols.

It has long seemed to me that these symbols may also be related to the different pictures of Jesus which the different Gospels present to us.

John himself, like an eagle, can be most vicious in attack, but Christ in the fourth Gospel soars to greater heights and sees far more clearly and widely than in the other three.

The obverse of a Roman coin carried a picture of an ox, standing in front of an altar and a plough; the inscription was 'ready for either'. This is so very close to the picture of Jesus which Luke gives us – the strong and gentle Suffering Servant, who is the Saviour of the world. A winged ox is the right symbol for Luke's Gospel.

However, I think the other two symbols would be better inter-changed to reflect the pictures of Jesus which those Gospels portray.

Mark presents us with a very human Jesus, who has familiar feelings and emotions like affection, anger, indignation, surprise, distress and agony. Mark vividly shows us the reality of the Incarnation, a Jesus who is one with us and who shares all our experience. A man seems a better symbol than a lion.

The Jesus of Matthew's Gospel is better symbolised by the lion than the man.

From its opening genealogy of Jesus and the visit of the magi onwards, this Gospel is very much concerned with the kingship of Jesus. The temptation narrative is deliberately cast in terms of Messiahship. More than any other, Matthew stresses that Jesus is son of David. Jesus has supreme authority over the Law. His kingship is evident throughout the Passion narrative in Matthew. This Gospel reads like the royal progress of the King of Love from Bethlehem to the throne of all authority in heaven and earth. Matthew portrays a royal Jesus, the Son of David, the Messiah, the Lord's Anointed, the Lion of Judah.

From this hypothesis, I see Year A (Matthew) as the Year of the King and the Kingdom, Year B (Mark) as the Year of the Son of Man, and Year C (Luke) as the Year of the Suffering Servant.

. . . continuing

YEAR A

THE YEAR OF THE KING
AND THE KINGDOM

THE GOSPEL ACCORDING TO MATTHEW

Matthew 7:21-29

The formula at the end of this and each of the other four blocks of teaching (Matthew 10; 13; 18; 25) is parallel to Deuteronomy 31:1, 24 and deliberately suggests that Jesus is the second Moses.

STANDING ————————————————

Jesus confronts you with a choice:

> which of the two ways? *
> which of the two kinds of tree? †
> which of the two foundations?

What matters most to Jesus
> is that you do what he says –

> for what you actually do
> shows what you really believe
> – no matter what you say you believe.

Foundations
Matthew carefully identifies the site;
> Luke concentrates on the foundations' depth. ‡

* Matthew 7:13-14   † Matthew 7:16-20   ‡ Luke 16:31-49

Whether you are building houses or character,
   foundations need to be sure and solid and unshakeable.

The Church needs its fundamentalists;
   but too often the Church is divided
   between radicals and fundamentalists.

Radicals are concerned with roots,
   reaching further into the depths,
   seeking nourishment, and strength
   and giving more stability to the living tree above.

The Church needs them both.

Standing

We need to know where we stand
   – *and stand there.*

It can be quite daunting:
   you may be Christ's only representative
   standing in that place:

   Remember, as Elijah was surprised to learn,
   you never stand alone; *
   and always there is One beside you
   who himself stood utterly alone.

In the storm

Matthew's description of the storm
   is more dramatic and frightening than Luke's;
   he is warning of the trials and tribulations
   that will accompany the coming of the kingdom.

* 1 Kings 19: 9-18

But how do you weather the storms of life,
   which are quite unavoidable for us all?
   What about unexpected storms on the sea of faith?
   Or when the sky is so dark that hope is almost gone?

Sometimes, all you can do
   is cling to the Rock of Ages
   by the 'skin of your faith's teeth'.

And if, for a while, you have no faith at all
   just keep on doing what Jesus says.

See also *Sunday by Sunday,* volume 1, page 95.

Matthew 9:9-13, 18-26

A meditation on the call of Matthew (Levi) and Jesus dining at his house is in *Sunday by Sunday*, volume 1, page 90.

LIFE AND WHOLENESS ─────────

Matthew studied Mark's vivid account
   and kept only what he regarded as essential
   in his most spectacular abbreviation,
   reducing twenty-three verses to nine,
   only 169 words instead of 466. *

No extra characters, no subplots, no crowds,
no names of the disciples or of the girl's father;

   but simply Jesus alone with the child,
   as had been Elijah at Zarephath, †
   and Elisha at Shunem. ‡

Nothing, for Matthew, must detract
   from the power of Jesus, son of David.

The hem of his garment
With a deft and familiar Semitic touch,
   Matthew also records that this desperate woman
   touched the tassel (the 'tzitzith') of his robe.

* REB † 1 Kings 17:19 ‡ 2 Kings 4:32

Hanging over the left shoulder,
    and reaching almost to the ground,
    it was made sacred by the interwoven violet thread,
    a visible reminder of God's commands. *

Not because she was embarrassed or shy,
    nor to avoid drawing attention to herself,
    but because she kept the Law,
    she approached Jesus from behind
    and deliberately touched the sacred thread.

Her sickness made her ritually unclean; †
    the Law would not allow her to approach him at all;
    but in faith and desperation she reached out.

No mention of any power gone from him;
    Jesus healed her by his spoken word.

Was the girl really dead?
Her father thought that she was dead;
    professional mourners had begun funeral preparations
    when Jesus strode into the scene.

Literally, the word he used implies a coma;
    he knew she wasn't dead;
    he always knows better than we do
    about our situations.

Left to those around her,
    the girl would have soon been buried,
    dead or alive.

But Jesus took her hand –
    and vindicated her father's implicit faith.

* Numbers 15:39 † Leviticus 15:25

Matthew's essential Gospel

More vivid details,
    such as Mark gives and Matthew omits,
    can bring stories of Jesus to life
    and have important meanings of their own;

    but in grief or anxiety,
    with incurable sickness, or in sheer desperation,
    come to Christ, directly or in secret:

His word can make you whole;
he and he alone can give you new life.

Matthew 9:35-10:8 (9-23)

FIRST APOSTLES _____

In the early days of his work in Galilee
    Jesus thought the Kingdom of God was very near;
    the urgency of the situation meant he needed help
    to announce its imminence to the people.

He appointed Twelve deliberately –
    a restored Israel would recover the twelve-tribe structure.

He shared his power with them
    so they could do what he was doing,
    their mission to extend his work,
    conforming to the pattern of his ministry.

Their initial mission was limited to Israel –
    but, as Matthew makes plain,
    it soon included Gentiles.

Having no luggage would affirm theirs was a holy mission;
    their poverty, like Isaiah's, was a sign of coming crisis. *

Rejection was as likely as acceptance;
    they must be prepared to withdraw from indifference
    – as later Jesus would himself withdraw.

* Isaiah 20: 2

They must expect no reward,
    'save that of knowing that they were doing his will';
    there was no place for avarice or greed:

God would supply their needs
    and they must trust him.

In this Gospel

Matthew deliberately groups the Twelve in pairs;
    but none of the gospel-writers agree about their names:

    why do we know so little about some of them?
    were some less popular or more self-effacing,
    or less prominent later?
    were some not with him all the time?

Matthew weaves into the mission charge to the Twelve
    other instructions and sayings of encouragement
    for those who suffered persecution in his own time.

Betrayed by families and friends,
    there was no promise of deliverance;
    like master, like servant,
    they would be as unpopular as their Lord;

    and they, like him, were in the Father's hands.

Matthew does not record the return of the Apostles
    for he is speaking beyond the Twelve to the Church:
    the mission is unending.

Some principles of Christian mission emerge

Mission must conform to the ministry of Jesus:
    the ministry of healing, in all its varied forms,
    has equal priority with preaching and teaching.

Mission, like charity, begins at home;
    how can you love the Africans whom you have not seen
    if you do not love your neighbours whom you have seen?

Mission needs a strategy of attainable objectives,
    excluding no one but proceeding by attainable stages.

There is no promise that we shall not suffer.
A servant is not greater than his master.

See also 'Come with me', *Sunday by Sunday,* volume 1, page 53.

Matthew 10:24-39

Matthew draws together further sayings relevant to the mission of the Church. Similarly, this meditation draws together various insights about Christian mission today.

MISSION IS ... _____

Essential

If there is no burning it is not a fire,
  if there is no mission it is not a church.

Christ has brought us together
  not for our own sakes
  but for the sake of this town (or village, or city)
  and its people.

Working with Christ

We are not called to take Christ into the world –
  he's there already!

We are called to recognise what he is doing
  and to share in it with him.

We are called and sent,
  as were the original Twelve,
  to be his representatives,
  to do what he is doing;
  ourselves to be as Christ to the people we meet.

Incarnational

Mission may often involve belonging to,
  and witness in, non-church groups,
  as salt and light and leaven.

Personal

Most people who go to church
  were first taken or invited
  by someone whom they know and trust.

Affirming

When everyone else said No to people's needs
  he said, and still says, Yes.

So many are depressed or deprived or rejected
  and need help to recover
  their sense of human dignity and worth.

Holistic

Man cannot live on bread alone
  – but he can't live without it either.

We are called to identify people's deepest needs –
  physical, mental, emotional, or spiritual –
  and move heaven and earth to meet them.

Reconciling

As the ultimate objective is the unity of all people,
  mission may well involve breaking down barriers –
  in the Church as well as in the world.

Sharing

On the Cross we find him where he always is –
    with the outcasts,
    alongside the suffering and the dying:

    we are called to enter into the fellowship of his sufferings.

Proclaiming

Through conversation or dialogue,
    or in drama, in sermon or in song,
    by silent integrity,
    and by selfless acts of service
    – all these proclaim the Kingdom is at hand.

Costly

There is no promise that we shall succeed.
There is no promise that we shall not suffer for it.

But this is our calling and the essence of the Church:
    a servant is not greater than his master.

Matthew 10:40-42

These verses conclude Matthew's section on Mission. Some scholars think there is also a reflection of the orders of ministry in Matthew's congregation.

A CUP OF WATER _____

A long, hot summer and a hose-pipe ban:
   we had squandered even our deepest reserves;
   we had been too cavalier with water
   – unless we had a meter!

Now with climate changes,
   and so much 'Yorkshire Water' weather
   and overflowing rivers, and worse that usual floods,
   it seems we have water and to spare.

Meanwhile . . .
   hundreds of African villages are desperate for a well,
   and every cupful, every drop, is precious;

   and 700 million people face a severe water shortage,
   not only in the Middle East and China
   but in parts of Europe too.

Giving
Just a cupful does not sound so very much to give;
   it's well within your capability:

He never asks for more than you can give.

For Jesus' hearers,
    a cup of water might involve a long walk
    and some sacrifice,
    but it was still within what they could do,
    to give sustenance to the weak and to the little ones.

For Matthew, the 'little ones' were God's 'ministers',
    and he urged his readers to welcome and support them
    with the promise of a share in their rewards.

For us today, Christ is calling
    in the cries of the thirsty,
    whose wells are dried up, or too far away,
    or whose water is foul and polluted
    following a natural disaster.

Still he asks,
    as he did by Jacob's well near Sychar in Samaria,
    'Can I have a drink of water, please?'

Inasmuch as you have done it . . .

Receiving
And what about the water given to you?

On that Friday afternoon,
    his parched tongue sticking to the roof of his mouth,
    he gasped, 'I am thirsty'.

One of the executioners,
    moved to compassion by his dignity in suffering,
    put a sponge on a cane, and held it to his lips.

Often help comes from the most unexpected people.

If you stumble and fall,
   and someone comes to help,
   you do not ask their religion, their politics or their name:
   you are simply grateful for their help.

Thirsty people do not care where the water comes from
   – if only it comes.

Thank God for all the people who have helped you;

Respond to every whispered thirsty plea for help.

And don't waste water.

Matthew 11:16-19, 25-30

COME TO ME _____

Early in the 1960s
    there was a revolution in religious education,
    led by men like Acland, Goldman, Loukes, and Hubery;

    the Christian content remained unchanged
    but they inspired new and better methods.

'Experiential education' caught on in the whole profession
    but, as so often with a revolution,
    the baby was thrown out with the bath water
    and, excited with the three Xs,
    the three Rs were often discarded.

In the inevitable backlash,
    the reverse has happened and, recovering the three Rs,
    many have forgotten that the only way we learn is by the Xs.

Learning of Christ

He invites us to come and learn of him –
    and the only way we can learn of Christ
    is how we really learn anything:
    by example, from experience, and by experiment.

You have learned so much from other people,
    from the example of parents, friends, and teachers:
    and you learn of Christ by following his example.

From the things that happen to you
  and from your own experience of life
  Christ has so much to teach you.

And you learn more of him
  as·you explore the truth – for he is Truth –
  and try to do what he says (experiment)
  and find it works.

There are four Rs: reading, writing, 'rithmetic, and religion:
  the fourth X is the way of the cross
  which you will learn is the way to life.

Follow his example, learn from what he shows you,
  seek the Kingdom of God and find the way of life.

Taking his yoke upon you
It's like standing with John the Baptist
  at the foot of a very high mountain.

A saint on the pinnacle calls down:
  'You ought to come up here – the view is marvellous!'
  the Baptist beside you insists,
  'Somehow you have to climb up to the top';
  and then Jesus comes alongside you,
  ropes himself to you, and says,
  'Come on – we'll tackle it together'.

And he is with you all the way,
  guiding you over the tricky bits,
  holding you safe if you stumble or slip.

Being 'yoked' to him
  means he is always alongside you.

You bring your burdens to him –
  he will not take them away

but will share the load
and the pulling is that much easier.

He will go at your pace and see you through,
    him keeping in step with you.

Being 'yoked' to him
    may also mean that you have to keep in step with him,
    following his lead, going where he goes.

Matthew 13:1-9, 18-23

THE MASTER TEACHER _____

There is no modern teaching method,
   tried and tested and proved effective,
   which Jesus did not use
   and at which he did not excel.

He taught them from the familiar things
   of their own experience,
   at home, at work, and in the family,
   from Nature and of human nature;

   sometimes he took the events of which they told him
   and showed them deeper meanings.

Adept at the Socratic method of question and answer,
   he welcomed and answered their questions;
   his own questions of them (and us),
   were always searching and demanded a response.

Equally at home with large crowds
   or in conversation one-to-one,
   he preferred small groups:
   so much of his teaching was in small groups,
   especially discussions over an evening meal –
   how effective were those first-century house-groups!

And supremely,
   in the tradition of the greatest rabbis,
   he excelled in telling stories;

they loved his stories,
and often, like children, wanted them repeated –
'Tell us again about the man who got beaten up.'

He told most parables to the Pharisees;
with the Twelve, his teaching was pure poetry.

He seized every available visual aid:
you can learn so much about God from what you see.

The sower
He pointed across the fields
to where a farmer was sowing wheat-seed, broadcast,
in readiness for next Spring's harvest festival at Pentecost.

The early Church treated parables as allegories
– so Matthew's explanation does not sound like Jesus;
but a parable has only one clear meaning
if you can discern it;
it is rarely allegorical.

Jesus was speaking of the varieties of response
to him and to his message.

This parable is most concerned
with the condition of the ground;
and though some soil in this story was receptive
much of the seed fell around the edge of the field.

It was a warning to the hard, indifferent, shallow,
to take seriously what he said,
and take his words to heart.

Though farming now is very different from then in Galilee,
the yield still depends on factors
beyond the farmer's control.

Years from now you may be surprised
   by an unexpected yield from a seed that you once sowed;

   but you will never know
   the total yield of all your labour;
   you too have little control over the soil;
   and the growing and harvesting are not up to you.

Simply make sure of the high quality of the seed you sow,
   and that you sow in faith
   and leave the rest to God.

Matthew 13:24-30, 36-43

The second of three parables about growing which lead this group of seven – reflecting Matthew's penchant for grouping.

Only Matthew records this parable – perhaps it was developed from the one in Mark 4:26-29; the added explanation is an allegory to meet some of the questions in the early Church.

AN EVIL TWIST ───────────────

Such vandalism was not unknown.
It was forbidden and punishable under Roman Law,
    as it is in India today.

Darnel grew as tall as wheat
    and, until the ears were filling, looked just like wheat;
    it was sometimes called 'bastard' or 'perverted wheat'.

Either for revenge or jealousy,
    meanness or sheer vindictiveness,
    the sole intention of such nastiness
    was to spoil the farmer's crop and yield.

Wickedness
The problem of evil is not explained
    but it cannot be ignored.

Evil is not eternal
    but the fact and power of it are plain:

there seems to be an evil twist
at the very heart of Man.

Patience

Their first impulse was to deal with it there and then
    but the farmer counselled patience until harvest;
    trampling down the good wheat would not help.

Sometimes good and evil look alike;
    and we are too quick to judge,
    too quick to label and to classify other people,
    and to want a purge.

Don't judge other people; only God can judge.
You won't know the truth about them until the End
    and then there will be some surprises.

You will be surprised to see some folk who are in heaven
    and equally surprised that some you expected are not there;

    and, as a famous Scottish divine once said,
    if you and I are there to see
    it will only be by God's surprising and forgiving grace.

The Good News

Darnel is darnel is darnel –
    without dramatic biochemistry it ever more will be so.

Weeds and wheat cannot change
    but people can.

Bad people can become good
    for God can forgive our sins
    and set us free from evil's power.

He can root out of us the things that spoil us,
   and help us grow in grace
    until we become what we are meant to be.

Equally, good people can become bad:
   pray earnestly, 'Deliver us from evil.'

Matthew 13:31-33, 44-52

Both Matthew and Luke (13:18-19) exaggerated about the mustard seed – it will never grow into a tree. Mark got it right (page 109-110).

PARABLES OF THE KINGDOM _____

Leaven

Leaven is not yeast but a home-made rising agent.

But it could so easily become tainted
　　and spread its poison through many weeks of baking
　　that it had become a symbol for the power of evil.

His enemies were startled by the image:
　　how could something evil represent the work of God?

The metaphor was well-chosen:

　　once leaven is mixed with the flour
　　it will keep on fermenting;
　　it sets in motion a disturbing process
　　that causes an upheaval, plain to see,
　　and transforms the whole into something new:
　　just like the Kingdom.

He was careful not to say
　　that this leaven was mixed or kneaded with the flour;
　　he said it was 'hidden' in the flour.

The Kingdom is hidden
　　just as the mustard seed and the leaven are hidden
　　(and indeed the hidden treasure and the undiscovered pearl)

　　but from such a humble
　　and insignificant beginning in Galilee
　　it will keep on growing and fermenting
　　till the sorting at the end of time.

The treasure and the pearl

Coming to faith for some can be quite unexpected,
　　like a labourer at his daily work, finding treasure in a field;
　　suddenly, and to their great surprise,
　　they meet the living Christ –
　　they never dreamed religion could be as real as this.

The parable is not about the ethics of 'finder's keepers'
　　but about the pure joy of finding the Kingdom
　　and what you will give up for it.

Many, like the merchant, yearn for such discovery,
　　searching long with many doubts and questions,
　　knocking and knocking and knocking
　　for the door to be opened.

Most of his disciples, with no such personal 'proof',
　　still seek his Kingdom, follow his teaching,
　　and stake their lives on his Truth;

　　they have slowly come to see
　　how they have grown and changed with him,
　　and that the joy and peace, the wholeness, is in believing.

Sought or surprising or still seeking
　　Christ is the chance of a lifetime.

But the price is high:
　　you don't get something for nothing.

The net

A past prime minister of Britain once said
    that the British Commonwealth
    is the greatest multi-racial community on earth;
    in that, as in other things, he was quite wrong:
    the Church is!

Matthew readily recorded another apocalyptic message
    to warn his own multi-cultural congregation;
    but the parable also stresses
    that, until the end of time,
    there must be no division in the Church.

This great multi-racial, multi-cultural community
    would never brag about being the greatest,
    and can never tolerate any prejudice
    against race or culture, age or gender.

God has no favourites.

The householder

Every good disciple, student and apprentice,
    finds new light in Christ.

But the new is not added to the old:
    notice that here the new comes first.

There is no need to give up what you had before
    but his new perspective has priority;
    all must be seen in his new light.

Everything now has its focus in Christ:
all our life-style and our traditions,
what we've always been and done
has to be re-interpreted in the light of the Gospel.

Matthew 14:13-21

This is the only miracle recorded in all four Gospels. Each writer tells the story with his own emphasis. We need to take account of both Matthew and Luke (9:12-17) but most scholars incline to the more militaristic implications of Mark's (6:35-44) and John's (6:1-13) accounts.

A DESERT MEAL _____

People from all over the region
    came flocking to find Jesus.

He wanted some prime time with the Twelve,
    but could not ignore the challenge of the people's needs.

He mingled with the crowds
    and healed many who were sick;
      but they wanted more than healing.

He stood on a small hillock and addressed them,
    his sure, strong, steady voice
      ringing over that vast crowd.

All day long he taught them truths about the Kingdom,
    and they hung on every word;
      until, in the evening, they shared that special meal.

Still he mingles with the crowds,
    still he is healing the sick;

no challenge is too great for him to handle,
no need too deep for him to meet.

Militant men

The thought of that great teaching occasion,
    and that special meal and miracle
    almost tempted Matthew to exaggerate:
    'not counting women and children' was true,
    but it implies there might have been ten thousand!

But most probably there were no women and children
    – only men, with a few adventurous boys;
    this was no Sunday-school picnic
    or a families' day out;
    the men were mainly zealots
    and they had come to fight.

Word that he might be the one to lead them
    had spread through Galilee like a fire;
    they had uncovered hidden swords,
    grabbed hold of pitchforks or sticks,
    and came eagerly to join him.

Five thousand faced Jesus at the lakeside,
    a crowd of excited, angry men,
    with the light of battle flashing in their eyes,
    with the hope of victory over Rome and liberty at last.

He stood alone.

He did not intend to fight
    or lead them into battle;

    but somehow he had to control that vast crowd,
    and calm their violent mood,
    yet keep alive their commitment to the Kingdom
    and sustain their longing for freedom.

He began (as always) where they were
    and treated them like the army they wanted to be:
    'Divide them into platoons,
    100 rows of 50';
    he stood before them like a general addressing his troops.

A special meal

He took the bread, said the blessing,
    broke the bread, and gave it to his disciples . . .

For first-century Christians, as for us,
    the words had deep significance:
    this was a sacramental meal.

They went home satisfied
    as you have done from such a meal;
    such satisfaction does not depend on a filling meal,
    a small piece of bread will do.

Calmer than when they came, they went home content:
    their hopes were sustained,
    they were pledged to each other in the fellowship of salt,
    the sacrament they shared looked to the coming Kingdom.

Prodigality

Symbolically, there was much food left over
    for God always provides more than we need;

    and if you challenge that with our world's starving millions
    he could still meet the needs of hungry crowds
    if he was given a chance.

Matthew 14:22-33

WALKING ON WATER _____

When a banner proclaimed
   'Ian Botham walks on water',
   it acknowledged a superhuman performance,
   that had seemed almost god-like.

'Walking on water'
   has become an accepted sign of divinity
   since the evangelists recorded this story –
   which is exactly why they wrote it down.

This sea was no 'mill-pond'.
Jesus must be God, striding across a tempestuous sea,
   making his way through the waters. *

Miracles
I believe in miracles.

I believe in the really big ones,
   the Incarnation and the Resurrection;
   I believe he healed the sick
   and cured the lame, the blind, the deaf, the dumb.

* Psalm 77:19, etc.

I believe in miracles
  but I do not believe in magic;
  there is no place for magic in the Christian faith.

When it comes to the 'nature miracles', however,
  I have to pause and wonder;
  but I'll keep an open mind.

A possible translation of John's version
  is that Jesus was walking *by* the sea and not on it.

The narrative

He had sent his disciples on their way
  while he went up the hillside
  to pray through his new problems.

In the light of the full moon of Passover
  he could see them quite clearly.

When they had gone about three-quarters of a mile
  dark clouds gathered and a wild storm broke;
  through a gap in the clouds,
  he caught a glimpse of them,
  struggling with the wind and waves.

His own needs were secondary now
  and he came to their fear and need;

  and they heard those strong, encouraging words,
  God's own name, coming out of the darkness:
  'It is I: don't be frightened.'

Simon Peter

Half afraid and half believing,
  Simon stepped out of the boat.

If this was really Jesus
> he was called to do what Jesus was doing.

Briefly he glanced away,
> and his faith wavered;
> he thought that he was drowning
> till Jesus grabbed and held his hand:
> 'You must keep your eyes on me.'

Parallels

He sends us forth
> and leaves us to get on with it,
> with the skills and strength we are already given.

But he cares for us and watches us
> and if we are in need he comes to our help.

If, like Simon,
> you want to be with Jesus,
> and to do what he is doing,
> as all disciples should,

> you'll be all right
> as long as you keep your eyes on him:
> faith depends on him from start to finish.

And hold on to that wonderful 'It is I':

> God in Christ is with you;
> even in the deepest darkness.

Do not be afraid.

Matthew 15:(10-20), 21-28

To travel from Chester-le-Street to Durham – take the A1 to Alnwick, then the coast road to Berwick-on-Tweed, the A1 back to Darlington, then via Sunderland, and so to Durham (at last).

REAPPRAISAL

It was a strange journey.
Follow it on a map of Palestine
   or find your own parallel (like mine above).

What was he doing?
What was going on?

Caution kept him away from Herod's lands
   where Herodians and Pharisees plotted to destroy him.

Galilee had not turned out as he expected:
   the Kingdom didn't come!
   they didn't really listen to what he said,
   and they wanted him to fight!

Incarnation does not mean
   that a lump of the Eternal was deposited in Palestine
   for men to look and marvel at.
Incarnation means that God became man,
   a living, breathing, throbbing, loving man,
   like us, not knowing everything,
   and having to learn from experience.

He reviewed his work in Galilee.
How could he make people take him seriously?

Had he been wrong and the 5000 right?
Would he have to take up arms?

He turned to those favourite prophet-songs.
Did it have to be the way of the Suffering Servant?

A Gentile woman
He was trying to keep to himself
   and pray through what he must do next
     when his thoughts were interrupted by a Gentile woman.

The woman was talking about her daughter
   but he was preoccupied with his own searching.
Should his ministry more deliberately include Gentiles?

His silence with her was not discourteous or unkind;
   he was wrestling with larger questions.

But the woman would not be deflected;
   one of those who would give as good as she got,
   she would not give up.

She knew he was not indifferent to her need,
   even though it seemed as if he didn't care.

She felt in her bones that he would help
   and she trusted him.

When she was nearly home, her daughter ran to meet her;
   he had healed her, of course – even at that distance.

Jesus
The Spirit that descended at his baptism
   was the Spirit of suffering love.

His decisions in the wilderness were confirmed,
   whatever had happened in Galilee.

He had to live and teach the way of love
   even though he might suffer for it.

A small shadow of a cross came to the back of his mind.

Matthew 16:13-20

A VITAL CONVERSATION ────────────

After his long re-thinking of what he had to do,
  Jesus took his disciples with him
  to the lonely places of the northern highlands.
He had so much to tell them.

This vital conversation, on which so much depended,
  proved to be a water-shed in his ministry;
  from that time on so much was different.
He had to bring into the open
  the differences between his understanding and theirs.

As they walked along,
  he asked what people said of him;
  and, though he was regarded as a prophet,
  significantly, no one thought he might be Messiah.

And then the crunch question:
  'What about you, who do you think I am?'

  and Peter, so quick it was almost automatic,
  'Oh we know,
  we know you're the Messiah.'

'Son of the living God' is not, as we might think,
  a recognition of Jesus' divinity;
  it was quite simply a Messianic title –
  they were quite sure that Jesus was the promised One
  who would lead Israel to victory and liberty.

And he told them to tell no one else:
   perhaps they had done enough damage already!*

The Church

The primacy of Peter
   is not in that he was the first to be called,
   the cleverest, the most cultured, or the wisest;
   but he had become the natural leader,
   he was chosen and appointed by Jesus,
   and in his preaching at Pentecost
   he was the first to witness publicly to the Resurrection.

The 'keys of the kingdom' are symbols of responsibility:
   authority in the Church is always about responsibility.

'The forces of death shall never overpower it'
   will encourage not only Matthew's persecuted readers;
   the Roman empire, and many others,
   have declined and fallen,
   the Jewish nation is dispersed,
   but the Church of Jesus Christ still stands and grows.

And whether you forgive or not has eternal significance.

Simon Peter

Simon is the sort of man
   that Jesus makes his Church of:
   a mixture of inspiration and self-interest,
   of insight and ignorance,
   of rock and sand.

* See page 45.

Sometimes with flashes of inspiration,
   sometimes the very devil,
   he is so reluctant to change his ideas
   and has still so much to learn.

He can make great promises of loyalty
   but can fall asleep and deny his Lord.

But he is capable of great courage and commitment

   – just as you are.

Matthew 16:21-28

FOLLOWING CAN BE COSTLY _____

He now spent most time with the Twelve.

He led them deeper into his truth,
    taught them of Abba and how to pray,
    about humility and the ways of the Kingdom.

That autumn, he did not know in detail
    what would happen the following March
    but the risk was ominously clear.

Now he began to teach them
    that the way of Love could become the way of suffering,
    for loving always involves suffering
    and it is costly.

'If you come with me
    you will have to be ready to die
    – for me and for the Kingdom.'

They had always known that they might be killed
    when they fought with him against Rome;
    but the emphasis now was different.

There and then it meant being ready to die;
    here and now it means 'dying to self';
    and it is still costly.

Dying to self

'Having a cross to bear'
    does not refer to a bit of rheumatism
    or an awkward relative
    but involves self-sacrifice.

It may well be that following him
    has proved more costly than you first thought,
    not only in time and money
    but in 'wear and tear'.

'Sharing the fellowship of Christ's sufferings'
    may involve facing apathy or ridicule,
    being misrepresented or abused,
    and it hurts.

It may well be that following him
    has not worked out as you expected,
    and this surprising Christ
    has led you in unexpected ways.

He still has much to teach you
    of his mind and of his ways.

Paraphrase

Alan Dale wrote this most perceptive paraphrase:

'If you want to help me,
    you must give all your heart to it.

You must put yourself last;
    you must be ready to let people do their worst to you,
    and you must keep your eyes on me.'

Keep your eyes on him.

Reprinted from *Sunday by Sunday,* volume 1, pages 114-16.

Matthew 18:15-20

In the early Church, as in any group of people, there were clashes of personalities and about policy. Just as Paul wrote to Corinth about divisions, so Matthew wrote into his Gospel clear rules about Church order.

IN HIS NAME ———————————————

The pattern of Church discipline
  which Matthew sets before his congregations
  has too often been distorted and abused.

It has produced puritanical witch-hunts
  (such as portrayed in Arthur Miller's *The Crucible*)
  and fostered most unchristian attitudes.

It has been seized by exclusive religious sects,
  with strict rules, rigidly enforced,
  and frightening attitudes.

Jesus had so many problems
  with rigid rules and regulations:
  always there must be exceptions.

Attitudes
The clue is in verse 17:

How would you treat a pagan or a tax-collector?
Shun him or exclude him?

How would Jesus treat a pagan or tax-collector?
   – never excluding or shunning,
   but accepting him, getting alongside him,
   befriending him.

He promised
   that when two or three are met in his name
   their requests will be heard
   and their judgements hold good.

It seems patently untrue.

So often we don't get what we pray for;
   but we neglect the key words
   'in my name'.

This is no magic phrase or formula
   to tack on to the end of our petitions
   to authenticate them and guarantee success.

In Hebrew culture, a 'name' reveals the character:
   so Abram becomes Abraham, Jacob becomes Israel,
   and Jesus is Saviour.

'In my name' means 'in my character';
   prayer 'in my name'
   means praying as he would pray,
   praying for what he would pray for.

So also 'judgements in my name'
   are based on how he sees people
   and how he would judge them
   – if at all:

   remember how he dealt with
   that woman caught in the very act of adultery.

All this means
  we have to see sinners and backsliders,
  any who offend against our rules and sensibilities
  as he sees them.

We need to know more clearly
  the heart and mind of Christ.

Matthew 18:21-35

FATHER, FORGIVE _____

A rabbi would advise, 'Forgive a repeated sin three times',
    so Peter thought seven times was doing very well;

    but Jesus would have no limits –
    'There must be no end to your forgiving'.

His first word from the cross was of forgiveness.

He saw it as the essential heart of the Kingdom,
    the only way for people to live together in peace.

He stressed its importance
    with the only couplet in his prayer:*
    if you are not willing to forgive another
    your heart is in no condition to receive forgiveness.
The barrier against your neighbour
    is also a barrier against God.

Forgiving
It can be very hard to forgive another
    especially when you've been very deeply hurt;

* Matthew 6:14

and even harder to forget –
much easier to keep score of the wrongs we have suffered,
festering deep in our memory, filed for future use;

easiest to say, 'I'll never forgive him for that',
but then you yourself will never be forgiven.

Forgiven

First, you yourself need to be forgiven;

God is ready, waiting,
   willing, wanting to forgive
   anyone,
   anything,
   everything.

It can be hard to accept forgiveness
   but it is the only way to the wholeness
   which is our deepest need.

It means admitting our fault
   and we are so good at making excuses
   and making allowances for ourselves;

   but we need to acknowledge our failure,
   honestly confess our neglect,
   our disobedience,
   our sin.

And we shall be made whole,
   given a new beginning,
   a restored relationship with God.

Forgiving

Now that you are forgiven
   this parable is for such as you.

It contrasts the astronomical debt that was cancelled
  with the trifling amount so violently demanded.

How he deals with you
  is how you should deal with others.

Give as good as you have been given.

Matthew 20:1-16

ACCORDING TO YOUR NEED _____

It wouldn't work in a market-place:
    the unions would call a strike;
    the next day everyone would come at five o'clock
    and work one hour for a full day's pay!

You'd be bankrupt in no time:
    it's no way to run a business.

But it's not about running a successful business
    it's about the Kingdom of God;
    God is like the owner of this imagined vineyard.

Different values

The one-hour workers had the same needs as the others:
    all needed to make ends meet.

He cared about them, their wives and children;
    he understood their needs;
    and he loved them –

    you can't divide love like sharing a cake:
    in a family of five or six or seven,
    each child is loved as much as if he was the only one.

The Kingdom of God has different values:
    the first is last, and the last is first;

the poor have priority – a bias to redress balance;
and there is no sneaking jealousy
of those who seem more fortunate.

The Kingdom of God is a family, a community of love.

A church should emulate the Kingdom:
    of course it must be run wisely and efficiently,
    but not to make a profit,
    even though they think we're always wanting money!
    It is not a business, nor dependent on market forces;
    a church is a community of love.

The principle from the parable is very clear:
    from each according to his opportunity
    (with so much unused ability it has to be 'opportunity')
    to each according to his need.

There is bad news:
'Can't I do what I like with my own money?' he said.

No, you can't!
It's not your money –
    for, if you are Christ's, your money is his.

You are no longer an owner
    but a steward – of all you think you own!
    All has to be used for him and his Kingdom.

But there is Good News
In the Kingdom of God
    you are given not what you have earned,
    nor what you deserve,
    but what you need.

It would be terrible if you got what you deserve,
    but you don't –

like the vineyard owner with his workers,
the Father is waiting to give you
what he sees you really need.

And if you accept what he is offering
you'll be back to work for him tomorrow.

Matthew 21:23-32

The first of three (another group of three) interlinked parables.

LET YOUR YES MEAN YES _____

The chief priests and elders had to respond:
  Jesus had thrown down a challenge they could not ignore.

They tried to trick him into blasphemy or treason.

But Jesus aligned himself with John the Baptist
  whom they had refused to recognise.

The two sons
These brothers are as different
  as were the sons of the prodigal father.*

The first, respectful and polite,
  made an automatic, superficial response
  and said he would obey his father;
  but he didn't;

  after his initial blunt refusal
  the second son changed his mind.

It is not what we say but what we do that counts.

* *Sunday by Sunday*, volume 1, page 136.

Lip-service or acceptable service

The priests condemned themselves by their reply.

They had ignored the demands the Baptist made
    while prostitutes and other blatant sinners
    had changed their minds, and changed their ways,
    and now had preference over priests for the Kingdom.

Some who seem irreligious in this unchurched generation
    by their loving commitments and generous deeds
    are nearer to the Kingdom than some 'churched'.

If up to now,
    you yourself have refused the invitation of the Father
    you can always change your mind;
    and turn your No into a Yes;

    or if your religious practice
    now seems no more than lip-service
    you too can change your mind
    and find true freedom doing what he says.

Saying Yes

It can seem easy to say Yes
    in the private stillness of your prayers
    or the security of a Sunday congregation,

    but be very different on a Monday morning
    in the cold light of day in a hostile world.

He insists you count the cost, as best you can,
    but be quite sure,
    he never asks more than you can do or give.

A perfect Son

There was also one son who said Yes
    and was as good as his word.

At his testing in the desert, he said Yes;
   and in Galilee, Samaria, Judaea, Ephraim,
   in agony of Gethsemane,
   and in the isolation of Golgotha
   he kept faithful and obedient to the Father.

Once committed, he kept on loving.

Say Yes to him –
   he is as good as his word.

Matthew 21:33-46

One story about a vineyard leads to another.

TENANTS FROM HELL _____

Isaiah's simple parable of the vineyard *
    is adapted and made almost allegorical;
    it is not difficult to identify who represents
    God, Israel, Jewish leaders, the prophets, and Jesus.

The tenants

Many rich Sadducees were absentee landlords †
    who could identify with,
    and would sympathise with, the landlord in the story.

They instinctively responded,
    angrily and violently, as many owners would,
    with how they would deal,
    or perhaps had dealt already,
    with such a situation.

Again they condemned themselves from their own mouths.

The cornerstone

The quotation from Psalm 118
    was quite a favourite in the early Church ‡

*Isaiah 5:1-7   † See page 262.   ‡ Acts 4:11; 1 Peter 2:7

70

though there is some uncertainty
about which this keystone is.

It might be either a foundation stone
or a large cornerstone which bound two walls together,
or even the coping stone which crowned the building.

Each is a fitting metaphor for Christ.

Christ is the only sure foundation on which to build
the only unshakeable rock on which to stand.

He can bind people together
and will bring all things to a final unity;
and he alone gives stability to his Church.

Christ is the crowning glory of his Church
and gives aim, objective and purpose to his people.

Conclusions

Matthew adds his own ending to this encounter: *
the new Israel has now replaced the old
and will be better, more obedient tenants.

Isaiah's parable stressed God's providence and care
but the fault was with the vines;
here the problem is the arrogance and greed of the tenants;
but tenancy still depends on fruitfulness.

The delayed return of the owner
and his repeated appeal to the tenants
is a reminder of God's patience with us and his grace
– but we must not take his grace for granted.

* Verse 43.

The vineyard is his not ours;
    we are but tenants in his world,
    and are accountable for our stewardship. *

The Church belongs to Christ and not to us:
    too often our councils and decisions
    suggest we think his Church is ours.

Our tenancy also depends on fruitfulness.

We are expected to grow
    – in numbers if we can –
    but at least ourselves in love and joy and peace
    and all the fruits of his indwelling. †

* See also pages 95-96. † Galatians 5:22

Matthew 22:1-14

This trilogy of parables (or are there four?) – Matthew 21:28
-22:14 – is in typical rabbinic mould: one story leads directly
into another.

THE WRONG TROUSERS _____

Why kill people for refusing an invitation?
Why mobilise the army and burn down their cities
   because they did not come?
Why bind and expel a man to outer darkness
   because he was wearing the wrong clothes?

It is all so very violent;
   and the punishments don't fit the crimes.

There is this dark and ominous theme
   which runs through Matthew's gospel.

The threat of the coming judgement of God
   is made in more than 50 places,
     with such phrases as unquenchable fire, eternal punishment,
     a furnace, and weeping and wailing and gnashing of teeth.

How different from Luke!
Matthew's version differs so very much from Luke's,
   not only in some key details but in style.

Matthew was concerned about his church –
    multi-racial and multi-cultural,
    a mixture of both good and bad
    (as were the wedding-guests),
    some with wavering commitment,
    some whose love had grown cold.

They knew they were the newly-favoured outsiders
    taking the place of those first invited
    who had dared to refuse the second call.

The fate of those who ignored the invitation was a warning,
    the burning city a reminder
    that Jerusalem had been burned,
    and the king inspecting the wedding-guests
    a picture of the imminent last judgement.

Matthew hoped all these repeated threats of judgement
    would urge his readers to firmer fidelity and obedience.

Many had been called but few of them were 'choice'.

That's the word Jesus actually used
    and, whether we feel threatened or not,
    we must admit few of *us* are, as yet, 'choice' Christians.

Wedding clothes
Why pick on one among all these down-and-outs?
No wonder he was speechless!

Not providing oneself with the proper clothes
    was thought to be as bad as refusing the invitation.
But had he tried? Did he care?
When challenged he had nothing to say.

It's about wrong attitudes, not wrong dress.

Years ago, to encourage a lad to come to a youth service
   I used a familiar ploy and asked him to take the collection;
   he came – wearing cords, a sweater, and wellington boots.

An over-zealous steward told him
   he shouldn't come into God's house dressed like that.

So he never came again.

You wear the best you can to come to worship
   but what matters most is the attitude in which you come.

Matthew 22:15-22

PRIORITY ————————————————————

Pharisees and Herodians were poles apart –
    any collaboration between them meant trouble;
    their question was as baited as
    'Have you stopped beating your wife?'

Jesus did not avoid the question
    nor leave the matter unresolved;

    he gave a clear-cut answer,
    affirming what Pharisees secretly believed –
    and exposed the hypocrisy of their question.*

The dilemma

We live in two worlds,
    as Matthew's readers
    and the followers of Jesus always do,
    citizens of two kingdoms,
    under two authorities
    which do not easily co-exist.

He seemed to suggest two loyalties
    as if your life is divided into compartments –
    home, work, social, religious, political;

* Verse 18.

but he above all others
wants you to be whole;

if your faith does not affect every part of your life
it won't convert a cat;
if your faith does not affect your politics
it isn't worth a fig.

Religion and politics

Moses laid the foundation
    with one giant ethical stride,
    joining religion and morality –
    attitudes to God and to your neighbour
    are two sides of the same coin.

Elijah was a great champion for human rights,
    Amos made plain God's predisposition for the poor,
    Isaiah counselled non-aggression,
    and so on through all the prophets

    till Jesus, appointing twelve apostles, *
    riding into Jerusalem
    claiming to be king.

All underline the principle:
    you cannot separate religion and politics
    – only a politician, nervous of the prior claim,
    would dare suggest you can.

The prior claim

The coin bears the image of Caesar
but a man bears the image of God
– and his is the higher claim.

* See page 23.

Give to God what is God's:
    but, for you, everything is God's,
    political obligation must be subject to him;
    absolute obedience to him has the first priority.

His servants can never sing
    'I vow to thee, my country . . .
    a love that asks no question!'

Jesus stands before Pilate
    (and Pilate is the one in chains),
    perhaps passive but never weak;
    he stands for truth and justice, integrity and compassion,
    and will not yield.

Be prepared to stand and not to yield.

Matthew 22:34-46

THE GREATEST COMMAND _____

It was a familiar question.

They loved to extend the Law
    to the minutest detail;
    although none could be the greatest
    for all were equally important
    and must be kept.

But of all 365 prohibitions
    and 248 positive commands,
    was there one basic principle
    which summarised them all?

Jesus answered as would any faithful Jew
    and reaffirmed their traditional faith,
    quoting the Shema which they recited daily, *
    and its counterpart recorded in Leviticus 19:18.

Two for the price of one
Asked for one basic commandment
    he gave them two.

He may not have been the first
    to summarise the Law in these two commands,

* Deuteronomy 6:4

nor the first to insist they stand together,
two sides of the same coin.

You can't fulfil either without the other.

He was *certainly* the first
to give such new depth and new intensity
to what Love means.

Understanding scripture

In turn, Jesus questioned them
and exposed the narrow and mechanical way
in which they interpreted scripture.

He used complex rabbinic arguments
which they understood quite well;
but it was clear he grasped the meanings
far better than they did.

Their silence was a clear admission,
as later Cleopas saw when walking to Emmaus,
that scripture must be seen *in his light*.

The Law, and the Prophets, and the writings
are a most precious heritage,
but all are pre-Christian, sub-Christian,
and sometimes quite un-Christian.

Sometimes even Gospels and epistles
may fall below his own high understanding.

Christ himself, and not the book, is the Word of God:
he speaks through the written word
though you may need to read between the lines!

You have to love God with all your *mind*
    and keep your wits about you.

Only if you read the Bible *in his light*
    will it come alive.

Matthew 5:1-12

WHAT YOU ARE MEANT TO BE _____

Every one of these sayings is so profound
   it deserves deep thought and meditation on its own;
   and each has suffered misunderstanding.

'Happy' is a poor translation for what Jesus said;
   Beatitudes are never as superficial as that.

Happiness is so very ephemeral;
   the pursuit of happiness can be a paper chase;
   blessed means being whole, content, your real self.

Every one of these sayings is so profound
   it deserves deep thought and meditation on its own.

The meaning of some words is very clear –
   words like 'merciful', 'hungering for justice', 'persecuted' –
   but others have suffered much misunderstanding.

Poverty is seldom 'holy';
   but Matthew makes sure you get the point:
   spiritual poverty is worst of all.

These 'sorrowful' are not enwrapped in their own troubles
   but are saddened into caring action
   by the sorrows of other people.

True meekness

We've been misled by 'meek and mild'
    to think of 'timid, nervous, wouldn't say boo to a goose',
    but meekness is not weakness.

Do you recall the chariot-race in 'Ben Hur',
    the rippling muscles and power of those fine horses
    all under the control of the driver's rein?
Arab stallions, once wild, dissipating their energies,
    now caught, trained, controlled,
    all that energy channelled in one direction?

Or think of a river in full flood,
    all that unharnessed power streaming to the sea,
    until the river is dammed
    and all the energy channelled for hydro-electric power.

That's the actual meaning of the word that Jesus used,
    that's 'meek'.

It means controlled and directed,
    not wasting your energies,
    but all your powers channelled in one direction.
    'Set your heart on his Kingdom . . .'

The pure in heart

When I was 11 I thought this saying meant
    that if I never had any impure thoughts
    through all of my life
    then when I die I would see God;
    otherwise ... that was a terrifying thought for a small boy!

It really means that if my heart and mind are pure
    I shall see God *now*
    in other people and in the things that happen.

There seems to be a media obsession
    with 'digging up the dirt' on every public figure,
    wanting to drag everyone down!

If you look for sleaze, you'll find it;
    if you dig for mud, it will stick – to you.

But if you look for good,
    if you look for God,
    you will see him – *now*.

It means learning to look as Jesus looked,
    having a heart and mind like his.

The peacemakers
Jesus did not talk of God's children
    but of God's sons!

It may irritate modern feminists
    but Jews then had no inclusive language;
    they had no word for grown-up, mature women –
    only the men counted!

Jesus was speaking of mature Christians,
    adult, fully-grown children of God;
    and they are, by definition and by nature, peacemakers.

We cannot be sure
    whether Jesus delivered all these sayings at once *
    but Matthew collected them together
    and set them in progressive order, like a ladder.

Get past the negative hindrances
    of self-sufficiency and self-pity,

* Luke 6:17

self-will and self-righteousness,
and you can become a channel
through whom forgiveness flows,
and, seeing God in other people,
share in his work of reconciliation;

then you will have become what you are meant to be.

The saints

Some whom we commemorate today were not perfect;
      but their martyrdom was an immediate path to glory.

Many were so Christ-like,
      in themselves and in their actions,
      that we celebrate their faithfulness and love.

All these challenge us to consider Christ's Beatitudes;
      and work at those where we ourselves are weakest

      until we too are so mature in faith,
      and so fully-grown in love
      that we can be called God's grown-up children.

A paraphrase

You will only be truly content
      and become what you are meant to be

      when you know that you need help
      from beyond yourself
      and accept it;

      when you are saddened into caring action
      by the sorrows of other people;

when all your resources are channelled
into the way of love;

when you work hard for justice and peace,
for the kingdom.

And you will only find inner calm and content

when you forgive
even those who have hurt you very deeply;

when love so works in you heart
that you can see God in other people;

when you work for reconciliation
wherever you see discord and division.

Then you will have become what you are meant to be

even if you suffer for it.

Another version of this paraphrase is in *Sunday by Sunday*, volume 1,
pages 59-60.

Matthew 23:1-12

DON'T BE LIKE THEM _____

> There was a little Pharisee,
> who had a large phylactery,
> right in the middle of his forehead;
> and when he was good
> he was very, very good;
> and when he was bad he was horrid.

Not all Pharisees were as bad as their reputation suggests,
> but for many their religion was more show than sincerity;
> and their name has become synonymous with hypocrisy.

Too often we Christians also are accused
> of not practising what we preach;

> and we all know only too well
> that too often the criticism is justified.

'Do as I say and not as I do'
> is not a Christian precept anyway.

'Do as Jesus says;
> do as Jesus did'
> is the basic Christian maxim.

Aids to prayer

The Greek word *phylacterion* meant fortification;
> the Hebrew word *tefillin* was rooted in prayer.

Phylacteries were small leather boxes,
    containing scrolls of texts from Exodus and Deuteronomy;
    a Jew bound one to his forehead and one to his left arm
    with narrow leather straps
    as Mosaic Law commanded, *
    and as an aid to prayer.

I may light a candle, as a sign of God's presence;
    I may look at a cross or icon to help fix my mind,
    I may use a 'holding cross', or tell rosary beads,
    but all these are only *aids* to prayer
    and have no magic merit in themselves.

Such aids can be most helpful,
    especially to a wandering or a troubled mind,
    but prayer does not depend on them.

Prayer is deep communion with God
    that fortifies and strengthens you
    for living in his way.

Against Pharisees

A Pharisee who wore phylacteries all day long,
    with broad bands to make sure that they were noticed,
    was publicly flaunting his piety;
    public admiration and authority seemed to matter most.

Matthew has attacked Pharisees throughout his Gospel
    and here has drawn together sayings of Jesus
    as a prelude to the violent and abusive tirade
    which follows this particular lection, †
    and which doesn't sound at all like Jesus.

* Exodus 13:9; Deuteronomy 6:8   † Matthew 23:13-36

He has expanded Luke's six denunciations, *
    added a seventh, and got so carried away
    that he got his facts wrong.

He wanted to warn his persecuted readers
    against confusing outer appearance with inner reality,
    against crimes committed in the name of religion,
    against abuse of authority.

The Church is egalitarian not elitist;
    its fellowship is grounded in equality;
    authority in the Church is not inherited,
    but earned by humble service.

The yoke of Christ

Jesus was angered by a legalistic religion
    which imposed so many rules and regulations
    that it became a burden;
    religion is supposed to be a joy and delight.

He will never ask of you more than you can manage,
    nor expect of you more than you can bear.

If you have collected other burdens,
    not of his devising or intention,
    he will help you carry them.

That's where his yoke comes in.

The heavy loads imposed by scribes and Pharisees
    are in stark contract to his yoke
    which is easy to wear and will not chafe your neck.

* Luke 11:42-52

He is there beside you,
   he yoked to you, you bound to him;

   you will try to match your step to his,
   but he will go at your pace,
   and if the going gets hard
   he shares the load.

Matthew 25:1-13

Emphasis on the Final Judgement with its rewards and punishments is a strong characteristic of Matthew's gospel. Scholars disagree whether this parable is a first-century allegory of the Second Coming.

WAKE UP AND WATCH _____

This vivid slice of village life,
    accurate to Jewish wedding customs in almost every detail,
    was well known to Jesus' hearers:

    bridesmaids with their torches,
    awaiting the bridegroom bringing home his bride;
    his arrival long delayed,
    probably by negotiations over the financial settlement;
    till they are roused to greet his coming,
    and lead the procession into the house and celebrations.

The door is closed

If Matthew's metaphor is right
    the foolishness of being unprepared
    is echoed in the ominous slamming of that door,
    when some are left outside.

Who would you expect to be shut out –
    paedophiles? terrorists? drug-pedlars? others?

What about people who have hurt you,
    people you don't like, or don't understand?
Who would you shut out?
Would you want to exclude any?

Do you ever wonder if you yourself might be excluded
    and end up on the wrong side of that door?

What really matters is whom God will refuse;
    will he exclude any?

People can exclude themselves
    and choose not to go in, of course,
    but all are welcome.

Coming – ready or not

After the Ascension
    the disciples expected the return of Jesus any day;
    but the days became weeks . . . months . . . years . . .
    and still there was no Second Coming.

How imminent was imminent?

This was before John's new theology and understanding
    that Christ is coming now.

The vivid story that Jesus told
    is not about being too late or being excluded.

It's about being ready
    for he is coming whether we are ready or not.

The parable calls us to be prepared,
    ready to recognise him when he comes,
    and to welcome him.

'Too late' may be the epitaph
   on many of the endeavours of the Church;

   but it is not too late for the Church
   nor is it too late for you
   to wake up and welcome and work with him,
   torches burning brightly with the flame of love,
   and with adequate resources of faith and love
   to be light for the world.

See also *Sunday by Sunday*, volume 1, page 15.

Matthew 25:14-30

In a fifth parable of the coming of the Son of man, once again the key figure is delayed, his sudden arrival creates a crisis, and divides others, setting fearful inactivity against positive action.

BONDSLAVES

Yet another story involves an absent owner.

The hidden God
Often it seems that God has gone away
    and left us to get on with it,
    almost as if he doesn't care;

    but his non-interference is necessary for our liberty
    and he is only hidden;

    and only hidden because we don't know
    how or where to look.

Although there are no signs, no proofs, no voices,
    he is closer than breathing, nearer than hands or feet.

The challenge
Avoid later English usage:
    the talents are not innate gifts or skills.

These slaves are given money –
    thousands of pounds, belonging to their master,
    to do with it what they could on his behalf.

The given amounts were disproportionate,
    as human abilities, circumstances and personalities differ.

Such responsibility proved too much for one slave;
    afraid of the risk involved, he played it safe –
    burial was said to be the best security against theft.

At the return and the accounting,
    he tried to excuse his own inept behaviour
    by shifting the blame on to the owner;

    trying to protect himself he lost everything:
    he who would save life will lose it.

His master was not as grasping as he said
    but proved most generous to his faithful servants.

Stewardship

This parable defines Christian stewardship,
    our stewardship of the earth,
    and of the Church,
    our stewardship of ourselves,
    and of all we think belong to us.

Everything belongs to God
    who trusts us to make good use
    of all the resources of his love
    which he puts at our disposal.

Don't clutch such treasure faithlessly,
    afraid of risking it
    or investing in other people;

and don't blame God for your failures or your fear.

Watching for Christ is not passive
    but active responsible service;

    and the reward is the opportunity for more service!

Matthew 25:31-46

THE PEOPLE'S KING _____

There is a dark and threatening theme
   running through all of Matthew's gospel;

     he emphasises the coming judgement of God
     with such haunting images as the outer darkness,
     Gehenna, tormentors, and perdition.

Matthew's concern was for the lapsed and back-sliders
   among his readers and in his congregation
   who were wavering under pressure from strict Jews;
   his book includes repeated warnings.

At times, he resembles a hell-fire preacher,
   dangling his audience over the pit,
   trying to frighten them into repentance,
   which is not the way to preach the Gospel.

The idea of eternal punishment for temporal crimes
   is quite immoral and no longer tenable;
   pictures of hell-fire are now equally void.

But our generation has lost its sense of sin,
   and sees little need to make recompense;

God is too often regarded as an easy-going Father
   who will let us get away with anything,
   as long as we say that we are sorry.

We are still accountable for our actions and inaction.

The King comes

When the King comes to his throne,
  in his surprising Last Analysis,
  the question is not about religious faithfulness
  but about what we have done for each other.

It would be quite mistaken to suppose
  that this reduces Christian faith
  to an extension of the Scout movement:
  'doing a good turn every day'
  or showing kindness to all in need.

The heart of Christianity
  is a relationship with God in Christ,
  a personal faith that proves itself by what it does;

  it would be equally mistaken to suppose
  that it is possible to help those in need
  without involving God;

  Christ is with and in every one of them
  and any response to them
  expresses and defines a relationship with him,
  whether or not it is acknowledged.

The people's King

A renowned American preacher has shown us
  that, if we take a pair of very sharp scissors
  and cut out from the Bible every reference to the poor,
  all that will be left will be like a piece of fragile lace.

Throughout all our Scriptures,
  God is predisposed towards the poor,

ranges himself alongside them,
and gives them priority.

This parable is true to the Incarnation
for the King is completely involved
in the suffering of his subjects;

and the King is also a shepherd
who cares so much about the least and the last,
that he is not only alongside them
but identifies himself with them –

serving him means serving them,
serving them is serving him.

Justification

In St Paul's great teaching about justification by faith
the scene changes from the courtroom to the throne-room
and the Judge does not pronounce a death sentence,
but the King declares an amnesty.

So, with Charles Wesley and the writer to the Hebrews,
we may boldly approach that eternal throne,
confident in what Jesus has made plain,
and in what he has achieved for us.

Judgement is, and will be, tempered with mercy.

But when at the last he catches our eye,
as he caught Simon Peter's across the courtyard,
and we see the same compassion and understanding,
and find forgiveness just as Simon did,

his first question could still begin,
'When I was hungry . . .'

. . . continuing

YEAR B

THE YEAR OF THE SON OF MAN

THE GOSPEL ACCORDING TO MARK

with a complement from

THE GOSPEL ACCORDING TO JOHN

Mark 2:23-3:6

Mark continues his collection of stories of scribes' objections. After complaints about the company Jesus kept and his disciples' neglect of fasting come two more about Sabbath-breaking.

LORD OF THE SABBATH ⸺⸺⸺⸺⸺⸺

This is much more serious than eating with sinners
    or ignoring rules about fasting;
    this is a matter of life and death.

The Sabbath is a central pillar of Jewish religion
    and Sabbath-breaking was a capital offence.

Walking through the fields,
    they were only doing what the Law allowed
    on any other day; *

    but this was the Sabbath
    and their 'reaping, winnowing, and threshing'
    were among thirty-nine specific forms of work
    forbidden on the Sabbath by scribal regulations.

This was not an emergency,
    nor were they starving like David's men; †

* Deuteronomy 23:25 † 1 Samuel 21:1-6

but Jesus claimed a deeper principle:
people matter more than rules and regulations.

A *traditional problem*

After months of careful planning
  a local ecumenical project hit an unexpected problem.

After worship on their first Sunday evening together
  the Methodist flower-lady collected the flowers
  to distribute to the sick;
  and the Anglican flower-arranger was appalled –
  those flowers should stay in church all week!

Fortunately they made the obvious compromise.

Your church needs to look beautiful and cared for
  whenever people come in;
  and should it not be open every day?

But we must always have care for those who are ill:
  human need has priority over tradition or regulations.

Entrapment

Pharisees and Herodians were also poles apart
  but, from the earliest days of Jesus's ministry,
  were plotting together to destroy him.

Imagine Margaret Thatcher working with Gerry Adams
  or Bill Clinton in close collaboration with Milosevic!

That's how much they were afraid of Jesus.

The man with the withered arm
  was clearly set up as a trap for Jesus;
  the authorities' only concern was to see
  if he would dare to heal on the Sabbath.

They might have known.

Jesus claimed the right to forgive sins, *
    to heal the sick and exorcise demons,
      and also the authority to interpret the sacred Law.

Divine Law or human traditions are only valid
    when they work for human well-being.

People matter most.

* Mark 2:10

Mark 3:20-35

THE FAMILY OF GOD _____

Contradictory rumours were reaching Nazareth.

Some were saying Jesus was out of his mind;
    others, using exactly the same forms of words,
    said he must have a special relationship with God
    to do what he was doing.

His family were naturally anxious about him,
    so they set out to bring him home.

Satan bound

A special deputation, sent by the authorities in Jerusalem,
    arrived to investigate Jesus.

His method of exorcising evil spirits,
    without incanting the names of many others,
    suggested he had a higher authority within himself.

Their accusation was ill-considered and illogical.

Jesus firmly pointed out how absurd it was
    to think that Satan would weaken his own Kingdom;

    Satan was strong, but was now securely bound,
    and his possessions were being plundered:

Jesus was setting people free
just as he still is.

Unforgivable sin

With great solemnity he stressed the warning
of the one and only sin that is beyond forgiveness.

His accusers were so arrogant in their own misconceptions:
they had decided that the Spirit at work in Jesus
was not Holy but of the devil.

They said black was white, good was evil –
and were so obstinate in their amorality
that they could not see any need to be forgiven.

That's the point –
forgiveness has to be accepted
or the offender remains unforgiven.

Here is your Father, grieving, aching,
longing to forgive you anything,
wanting to forgive you everything . . .

but if you do not see the need
and will not accept his offer of forgiveness
he cannot set you free.

The family of God

His family waited outside
and had to send a message in to him;
they were not within the circle of his new community.

Some of them were hurt by his response;
some, who probably thought he never should have left,

wanted to take him home by force;
but his mother understood.

She remembered his delight in the joy and security,
in the love and caring of their nuclear family –
and he wanted that experience for everyone,
to extend it till it encompassed all people.

Calling the Church the family of God
may cause difficulties for some,
especially those whose own family experience is painful,
but what other description will serve better
when God is Abba?

Christ is our brother,
and he gives us to each other
to enjoy each other's lives
and grow through each other's love.

It is not always like that:
some funny people go to church,
few are saints, all are sinners;
you may even manage to get in and out
without anyone speaking to you!

He expects his Church to be a community of love.

Just as he promised Peter, *
I have known some wonderful 'fathers in God',
been 'mothered' and nurtured in the Church,
and have so many brothers and sisters.

* Mark 10:29-30

Haven't you?

As always,
    Christ keeps his promises.

Mark 4:26-34

There is no parallel to the parable of the growing seed in other Gospels though Matthew 13:24-30 may be an extension of it.

QUIETLY GROWING _____

Jesus was not trying to be obtuse
    or to conceal the truth form earnest seekers,

    but his parables might have confounded his enemies
    who scrutinised his every word.

The parables were simple analogies and comparisons,
    drawn from familiar experiences of daily life;
    each had one essential meaning,
    each reflected one facet of the mystery of the Kingdom.

Secret growing

Once the seed is sown
    even the best farmer cannot control its growth
    or predict the size of harvest.

Growing is imperceptible and secret,
    and yet so certain that it seems almost automatic:
    God alone controls the process.

Similarly the prodigious growth of mustard seed
    is by the power of God.

The mustard seed

A mustard seed will grow into a shrub,
   perhaps three metres high,
   but it will never become a tree;

   birds will perch on its branches
   but they will never nest there.

Some inferred a prophetic reference –
   for a mustard bush does not compare
   with a towering cedar atop the highest mountain,
   such as the kingdom Ezekiel promised *
   and they all hoped for.

Mark intended that the roosting birds
   would reflect the universal nature of the Church.

But the most obvious meaning is the contrast –
   just as a microcosmic seed grows to an enormous bush
   so also does the Kingdom grow.

From such small and insignificant beginnings in Galilee
   it will keep on growing.

A growing church

Your own experience of the Church may question that.

Religious practice has declined in western Europe
   after two wars exposing superstitious heresies
   and two generations obsessed with monetary policies,
   but there are now signs of some spiritual re-awakening.

The Church is growing as prodigiously as mustard
   in Africa, and South America, in the Far East,
   and now again in Russia.

* Ezekiel 17:23

And that's only the Church Militant!

The Church Triumphant does not lose its members
  and so is bound to keep on growing.

There is no need for us to worry
  what will happen to the Church when we are gone –
  it will still be growing.

If the last 50 years are any indication,
  in 50 years from now
  the Church will be very different from what it is today,

  but it will still be growing –

  as long as it serves the Kingdom.

Church and Kingdom
We must not equate the Kingdom and the Church
  for they are not commensurate nor identical.

It is possible to be a servant of the Kingdom
  without belonging to the Church;

  and to be a member of the Church
  but not a servant of the Kingdom.

Although the church is growing,
  it is the Kingdom that is like a mustard seed
  and the Kingdom must have priority.

Mark 4:35-41

IN A STORM ─────────────────────

He has never done that for me!

There have been a few storms in my life;
    times when dark clouds have gathered,
    and my sky has gone black;
    my little boat has seemed about to sink,
    and I've been very frightened.

I've cried for help:
    but he didn't seem to hear or care;

    and never once did he dispell the storm
    with a commanding word.

I've had to hang on
    by the skin of my faith's teeth
    till the storm had passed.

The absent God
It seems to be a common experience:

    God can seem very near,
    but more often far away,
    or even non-existent;

    mostly God is 'hidden'
    and sometimes very well hidden indeed.

Then I came to see
    that he was in my boat with me.

I have to look at what this story means
    in the light of my own experience,
    though trying to explain it
    must never mean explaining it away.

Gospel writers used the story as a proof of his divinity
    and that he is Lord of nature.

It doesn't prove anything for me
    though I'll keep an open mind.

I can never believe in magic,
    but I believe in miracles
    although miracles do not have to be spectacular.

Calm in the storm

Jesus asleep in the boat
    is a symbol of serenity and calm,
    not that he doesn't care.

Whether he calmed the winds or not,
    he certainly calmed his disciples.

That's the miracle for me –
    that Christ with his peace
    was with them in the boat;

    and he is in my little boat with me,
    with me in the midst of the storms,
    and he can give me peace.

We don't trust him enough.

Reprinted from *Sunday by Sunday,* volume 1, pages 92-94.

Mark 5:21-43

This must be the most-quoted indication of how Matthew abbreviated Mark's account (466 words reduced to 169) and of how closely Luke's telling follows Mark's whose additional information and more dramatic story has its own significance.

HEALING AND WHOLENESS _____

In the middle of this surging crowd
   suddenly Jesus stopped
   and asked who had touched him.

It seemed a silly question
   with so many jostling round him.

Perhaps you too brushed against him
   in your travelling today
   without realising who it was –

   but if you will make time to stop and retrace the day
   you may recognise when and how he came to you.

Not magic but faith
I get the clear impression
   that Jesus would have waited all day long if need be
   till he knew who it was.

He felt power draining from him
    (just as blood drained from the woman),
    but there is no room here for any superstition:
    Jesus is no magic miracle-worker.

The whole point is that he does not do magic,
    has neither magic clothes nor magic hands.

Again and again this gospel stresses
    it is faith, and faith alone, that makes you whole.

At the house

The people were as tumultuous as a stormy sea
    till he told them also to calm down.

Beside the young girl's parents,
    Jesus took with him only Peter, James and John,
    these three who became his closest friends,
    who also witnessed his agony in Gethsemane,
    the glory of his transfiguration,
    and here his power of resurrection.

I sometimes wonder if Andrew felt left out?

Being a disciple of Jesus needs humility
    as well as sharing his agony and glory
    and knowing the power of his resurrection.

In Mark's Gospel

The two narratives are interwoven and interdependent.

Both a pillar of the establishment and a social outcast
    can come to Christ for help.

Twelve years links the woman with the girl,
    both by their sickness were unclean,
    and both were restored to well womanhood.

Resurrection is shown to be simply an awakening.

Jesus wanting the girl to be fed
    stresses the reality of her restoration
    and his continuing concern.

Mark 6:1-13

A NEGLECTED MINISTRY _____

He sent them out to preach and to teach,
  to heal the sick and deliver people from their demons.

The Church has the same commission.

We maintain a proper emphasis on preaching the Gospel
  though we are losing our way in teaching the faith;

  we still campaign against what hurts, divides, destroys,
  but we have neglected the ministry of healing.

Healing ministry
If you are sick
  go and see your doctor!

Doctors are the front line
  of Christ's healing work today;

  so are nurses, consultants, chemists,
  psychiatrists, midwives, and paramedics;
  health visitors, and hospice and home carers
  – and all whose skill and dedication
  he can use in making people whole.

He urges and inspires
  transplant and keyhole surgery,

new discoveries, medical drugs, techniques;
some for diseases he could not have named
– but all these new techniques are his,
part of his ministry of healing now.

Church and healing
His Church too has a vital role
   although too long neglected.

Every congregation is supposed to be
   a healing-place where people are loved and accepted,
   affirmed, enabled and encouraged.

Every act of worship, especially every eucharist,
   is a place of healing.

As four men brought their friend to Jesus,
   we too should bring others in faith to him:
   we need more cells for informed prayer.

We also need time together
   to work out what those prayers mean
   that we ourselves have to be and do
   as part of the answer for which we pray.

Still the Church must lead the fight
   against all that hurts, divides, destroys;
   and encourage all that heals, creates, makes whole.

Healing and wholeness
Services especially for healing and wholeness
   are essential in this ministry;

   but many Christians are apprehensive,
   fearing uncontrolled or extravagant excess.

I must bear witness
    that in such services I myself have found
    more calm and peace than in any other place.

Seldom do people throw away their crutches;
    he may cure infirmities or he may not.

At Nazareth

They were proud of him in Nazareth
    when they heard that one of their own lads
    was becoming so well-known.

It was different when they saw him:
    surely they had taught him all he knew
    – he was getting above himself.

Familiarity bred such contempt
    there was no question of any mighty works.

Mark in this Gospel insists
    that healing and faith are inseparable,
    that if you trust him he will make you whole.

If you come trusting him
    and are not cured
    it does not mean your faith is lacking;

    he never promised to cure you
    though he might;

    he promised to make you whole
    and he will.

Mark 6:14-29

Many preachers will take one look at this reading and turn quickly to the day's appointed Epistle or Old Testament lection but this narrative has its own significance, especially for Mark.

FAITHFUL UNTO DEATH _____

Mark used this unexpected interlude
  to link with the conversation at Caesarea Philippi,
  and to stress the importance of John the Baptist.

Not only as a voice crying in the wilderness
  did John prepare the way for Jesus;
  what happened to John the Baptist
  also foreshadowed what would happen to Jesus.

Both were arrested,
  both sentenced to death
  by rulers who were hesitant before their goodness
  but still condemned them to please other people;
  both men's disciples took and buried their corpses;
  both were said to have risen from the dead
  but there the likeness ends:

  the rising of John was no more than empty rumour
  but the resurrection of Jesus was certain and true.

Herod Antipas

The family of the Herods were infamous
    for incest and lust, intrigue, murder and corruption.

John had fearlessly denounced
    the adulterous marriage of Herod Antipas *
    – Herodias was his wife and niece and sister-in-law!

She would never forgive John for what he said
    and was determined to have vengeance.

Herod was desperate to keep his power,
    and indulge his appetites;
    he was torn between the good he recognised
    and the bad he was encouraged to do;
    haunted by the guilt of killing John the Baptist,
    he had a superstitious fear of retribution.

Jesus and Herod

When Herod began to show an unhealthy interest
    in what Jesus was doing –
    'It's like that John the Baptist all over again' –
    it was time to be wary of the sly old fox.

For months Jesus avoided any unnecessary risk
    and carefully skirted round Herod's territory.

There is always place for proper discretion:

    early Christians soon stopped seeking martyrdom,
    even though it guaranteed a place in heaven –
    they did not want all their leaders
    in the Church Triumphant!

* Leviticus 20:21

Jesus knew his time had not yet come –
  the Twelve were not prepared nor ready to be left,
  and Jerusalem had to have the same chance
  to respond to him as he had given Galilee.

When all that was done,
  he would stand as fearlessly and unflinchingly as John
  before Herod – and Caiphas – and Pilate.

A time to stand
Avoid the sins of Herod Antipas and of Herodias.

In the licence of a permissive society,
  unshackled by a sexual revolution,
  Christians need to know where Love stands
  and to stand there.

God expects us to be discreet
  and not to take foolhardy or unnecessary risks,

  but when there is need to stand
  for justice or truth or love
  he asks that we stand as fearlessly as John.

Honour John the Baptist and all martyrs

  and pray for all who suffer for the Gospel's sake today.

See F. Pratt Green's great hymn 'Pray for the church, afflicted and oppressed'.

Mark 6:30-34, 53-56

RIGHT TEXT, WRONG SERMON _____

Jesus sent out his disciples at least twice,
    three times if Luke's mission of the 72 is right.

On Easter night,
    he said 'As my Father sent me, so I send you . . .'
    – he could well have added,
    'and I hope it works better this time!'

The first mission had the most undesired effect.

Back from mission
When the apostles returned they were so excited,
    and thought it had been a great success. *

But was he less than enthusiastic?
    I sense irony in his response
    'Oh yes, I saw Satan fall!'

Had it all gone wrong?

They told him what they'd been doing;
    we can only look at the results and guess!

* Luke10:17, 18

Suddenly, all over Galilee,
   there was such a buzz of activity
   that Herod got quite worried.

Jesus wanted to take his apostles away
   for a rest and some peace and quiet,

   but they were met by an army of 5000
   – and that was the last thing he wanted!

If the Twelve had caused all this,
   what had they been doing?

Perhaps they took his message, as he directed,
   but preached their own unchanged ideas
   – his text, their sermon:

   'The Kingdom of God is at hand'
   and we have found Messiah.

Since they were very small,
   they had been taught Messiah would lead an army.

If they did proclaim their ideas and not his,
   their dreams not his,
   their kingdom not his,
   no wonder the crowds came flocking!

This may simply be conjecture
   but too many of his heralds
   have used his words as a peg
   on which to hang their own unchanged ideas.

Not as God thinks
They didn't really listen to him
   but jumped to their own conclusions.

I've done it myself;
   and suffered it in others far too often.

Christian people with unchristian attitudes –
   church on Sundays and ungodly things on Mondays,
   – some even on Sundays may compromise their Lord
   before they've left the porch!

It's so easy to be called by his name
   and not really listen to what he says,
   or think through the implications,
   and still cling to our old unchanged ideas.

John 6:1-21

Gospel readings for today and the next four Sundays are all from John, chapter 6. John does not record the Institution of Holy Communion in the Upper Room because he has already said all he had to say in this profound and mystical chapter.

Each of these five pieces includes one present understanding of the Eucharist.

FEEDING THE CROWD _____

It would have taken at least ten hours
    for Jesus to give everyone a piece of bread
    if my experience in serving is anything to go by!

They would certainly need the Passover moon,
    for it would be very late before he finished.

John sets Jesus on a higher plane than any other:
    for him, Jesus who is himself the bread
    must serve all the people.

The boy's offering
The lad whom Andrew found and brought
    did not offer to *share* his food with Jesus –

'Would you like two or three of my loaves
    and one of these two fish?'

He offered all he had.

Do not offer to let Jesus share you life –

    put all you have at his disposal:
    heart, and mind, and soul, and strength;

    give all to him
    and the miracle begins.

At Holy Communion

The people were asked to sit down as at a banquet
    and the symbolic meal they shared looked forward
    to the coming of the promised Kingdom:

    Holy Communion always has that future dimension,
    proclaiming his death 'until he come',
    looking forward to the marriage supper of the Lamb,
    the great feast he has prepared for all people.

When John insisted that Jesus served the people
    he stressed a most precious truth:

    when you come to Communion,
    whoever gives you a piece of bread,
    it is Christ himself who comes to you,
    and serves you,
    and your Communion is with him.

For verses 1 to 13 see also 'A desert meal', page 44.
For verses 16 to 21 see 'Walking on water', page 47.

John 6:24-35

GREATER THAN MOSES _____

Moses has had more influence
　　on human history and individual lives
　　than any other man – save Jesus.

He came to a crowd of slaves
　　in the name of an unknown, invisible god,
　　and evoked enough trust for them to follow him.

He led the Exodus,
　　forged and founded Israel,
　　established a Covenant people,
　　carved out the Law for their life together
　　and much more besides;

　　and on every count
　　Jesus is greater than Moses.

He brought a new deliverance,
　　founded a new Israel,
　　with a new and positive Law,
　　and established the new Covenant
　　through which God can work in our hearts and lives.

Hunger for life and love
Jesus began where the people were –
　　with their daily labour.

Life is more than food to keep you alive.

You are body, mind, and spirit,
    and if you neglect any of that trinity,
    you are not whole.

I can see a netted fish on a river bank,
    gasping and gulping for life,
    completely out of its element;

    and I worry
    about those who deny any spiritual dimension,
    or are so obsessed with their physical needs
    that they neglect music, poetry, beauty, prayer,
    or any of those things that feed the soul;

    for when they come to the next stage of life
    in a world that is only and entirely of the spirit
    they will be completely our of their element.

Jesus, urging them to work for food that lasts,
    was preparing them to understand the truth
    that by his death and resurrection they will find life.

The spiritual equivalent of earning your bread
    is simply trusting this same Jesus.

At Holy Communion

There may be a time when you do not hear
    what God is saying to you through the sermon,
    or the music, or the prayers –
    and you've missed it!

There are five doorways to your spirit
    and one of the blessings of the holy sacrament
    is that it employs all five of your senses –

and if God can't get through to you by one door
perhaps he can by one of the others.

Holy Communion has sure links with the past
as well as with the future.

When the minister or priest
puts the bread into your hand
for that brief instant you are physically joined
just as you are spiritually joined by Christ.

You are also made one
with all the other communicants;

and beyond that building
Christ joins you with all his people on earth,

and in the mystery of this blessed sacrament
you are joined with all who have gone before you

and you are one with Moses,
and Elijah, and Isaiah, and Jeremiah,
and Andrew and Simon, and James, and John,
all apostles, and prophets, and saints, and martyrs;

in this sacramental bread
he joins you with all who have gone before us,
and with all those you know and love
who are for now beyond our horizons.

With such profound nourishing of the soul
we, like those men by Galilee,
go home satisfied.

John 6:35, 41-51

I AM THE BREAD OF LIFE _____

Here is the first of the magnificent seven great I AMs
    which are threaded through John's gospel
    like a string of priceless pearls.

Using the most sacred and personal Name
    which God had declared to Moses
    and which was too holy for any Jew to speak,
    Jesus claimed his own unity with the Father.

No wonder they disapproved and grumbled;
    it was blasphemy to use the Name of the Most High
    and how could he have come from heaven
    when he had human parents?

I AM confronts us with the Incarnation,
    the mystery beyond our grasp,
    the very heart of Christian faith.

God, who gives us daily our bread,
    is so committed to us
    that he was in Christ –
    and Christ alone can feed us,
    nourish and sustain us in both soul and body.

Eternal life

Christ offers life that is eternal
not only in quantity but in quality,
not only in length but in depth.

The life he offers is not only everlasting
    but of that permanent and stable quality
    which cannot be overwhelmed
    by any circumstance or suffering or evil.

We make the love of God too narrow;
    we put false limits on the scope of resurrection;
    and our ideas of life eternal are too small.

Truly, most importantly, he did not say
    that a believer *will* possess eternal life
    but that a believer possesses it. *

Eternal life begins before you die;
    here and now Christ offers a new lease of life;

    we have passed from death to life already,
    but only by the costly sacrifice of Jesus.

At Holy Communion

They broke bread as he had commanded them,
    simply in obedience, and as a memorial.

But it was as if they were in that upper room again,
    him talking of his body being broken and his blood shed;
    it was as if they were kneeling by that cross at Golgotha;
    it seemed like Easter night again,
    him breathing his peace over them.

It was all so vivid, so very real.

It is his 'real presence'
    that has made sharing bread and wine
    central to Christian worship for two millennia.

* Verse 47.

It is just the same for you
    when you come to Communion –

    as if you share that Passover in the upper room,
    as if you are kneeling before the cross
    where all sins are forgiven,
    as if it is Easter and the living Christ is come to you.

In this Holy Communion
    you are come to the presence of the living Christ,
    to a liberating new lease of life,
    to life eternal now.

John 6:51-58

The dialogue, which in John's Gospel has developed from the sign of feeding the crowds, comes fully to its climax in teaching about the eucharist.

BREAD OF HEAVEN —————————

A steward invited us to offer our gifts to God –
   the money was collected,
   prayed over by the minister,
   and placed upon the table.

I was only a child
   and watched to see God coming for his present –
   but he didn't!

(I did see that steward get it and take it away!)

Later I understood
   that the money which we offer to God
   he gives back to us to use for his sake and Kingdom;
   it has been given a new significance.

At Holy Communion
We bring bread and wine as our offering.

Bread is a symbol of our daily life,
   all we have and are,

all our gifts and skills,
   all the life that God has given us.

Wine is red like blood,
   a symbol of our suffering and need –
   and to whom else can we bring it
   but to Christ?

When we offer bread and wine to him,
   in those symbols we are offering ourselves,
   all our life,
   all our need.

And he does with the bread and wine
   what he does with the money:
   he gives them back to us –
   but they have new purpose.

Transignification
The bread is still bread
   but it has new meaning:

   as we receive it back
   we are no longer thinking of our daily life
   but only of him,
   and his suffering for our sake.

The wine remains wine
   but is has a new significance:

   as we receive it back from him
   we are no longer thinking of our own needs
   but only of him,
   his blood shed for our healing,
   the new Covenant he has achieved for us.

The bread tastes like bread,
    the wine tastes like wine,
    but their meaning has been changed.

Sometimes you will be sure of his real presence,
    sometimes you may feel that nothing has happened,
    but feelings can be most unreliable.

You have done what he commanded
    and he has done what he promised.

Christ has come to you
    with his healing and his life and his love.

The promises are true.

Self-offering
Offer your whole self to him
    and he will do with you
    what he does with the money
    and with the bread and the wine –

    he will give your real self back to you
    but with a new significance,
    a new meaning for your life
    and a new purpose.

John 6:56-69

This is the parallel in John's Gospel to the conversation at Caesarea Philippi in the synoptic gospels which marks the end of Jesus' public ministry in Galilee.

NO OTHER NAME OR HOPE _____

Jesus was talking of spiritual food.

As in the Eucharist
 bread and wine become part of your physical body,
 so Christ becomes part of your life,
 and is with you and within you.

But eating flesh sounded like cannibalism to some;
 drinking any blood was anathema to a Jew;
 it was more than they could stomach! *

And when he claimed equality with God
 and then questioned their belief in him,
 they'd had enough.

The Galilean ministry was coming to an end:
 in Mark's gospel Jesus left the people, †
 in John's the people moved away from him.

*NEB † Mark 7:24

To whom else?

It was not working out as the Twelve had expected;
  though they still hoped to lead the big battalions
  and after the victory be in the best seats.

They saw the crowds melting away
  and his popularity decline;
  but where else could they go?

Some things he said were hard to understand
  but they were sure he was Messiah.

He had a presence and a power that held them;
  his words had the ring of truth;
  he had the secret of being really alive;
  and they had never met anyone else like him.

It may not have worked out as we had expected either,
  since we first called him Lord.

We have seen many others go away
  but we want to keep on following him.

We have caught his vision,
  have learned so much as we travelled with him,
  and trust his promises;

  to whom else could we go
  for such life and light and love?

The sacrament of Holy Communion

The Victorian recruiting sergeant sat in the market place
  and put a shilling, one day's pay, upon the table.

No matter if a man could neither read nor write,
  there was no deed or contract to sign;
  all that was needed was to take the 'Queen's shilling'.

Picking up that one day's pay
    was an oath of allegiance:
    Yes, I will join the army;
    I am prepared to give my life for Queen and country.

In exactly the same way, a Roman centurion,
    recruiting for the army that maintained the empire,
    would offer one day's pay.

Simply by picking up that coin
    a man was making a similar oath of allegiance
    to the Roman emperor and his empire.

That coin was called a sacramentum.

Holy Communion involves a similar vow.

You come with open hands and open heart,
    wanting, willing to receive
    all that Christ alone can give;

    and you pledge yourself to him
    to his people and to his Kingdom.

Yes, Lord, I offer my whole self to you;
    I will do what you say,
    I will go where you send,
    I will give my life for you, my Lord,
    and for your Kingdom.

Mark 7:1-8, 14-15, 21-23

IT'S ALL IN YOUR MIND _____

A lovely-looking girl got on the bus
    and most heads turned.

She had a classical beauty and figure,
    and was most attractively dressed.

The faces of other passengers
    registered a wistful pleasure or delight
    – until she began to speak.

Her voice was like the voice of many cement-mixers,
    coarse and loud and grating;
    and the content was worse than the intonation,
    crude, judgemental, blasphemous;
    it was a real turn-off.

If only she had given as much care to her attitudes
    as to her appearance!

Man-made laws
Pharisees were most zealous in religious observance;
    they were not all nit-pickers or pettifogging lawyers;

    but when hungry disciples ignored a traditional ritual,
    the Pharisees were quick to attack Jesus through his friends.

Jesus made no defence of his disciples,
  but launched a scathing counter-attack on their accusers,
  contrasting appearance with reality. *

He opened up the whole debate
  about the validity of traditions;
  minute regulations can often obscure the real principle.

He contrasted the eternal law of God
  with man-made laws which are not sacrosanct.

Simply because it seems good to us
  or we've always done it that way
  does not mean it can never be changed
  or has Divine approval.

The heart of the matter

With the crowd and later with this disciples,
  Jesus explained the truth about uncleanness
  and what really defiles a man or a woman.

His appalling catalogue of sins and crimes,
  repulsive to us all,
  are all actions of an unclean mind and heart,
  not anything external;
  and they all can seed and reproduce themselves.

The heart of the matter
  is a matter of the heart and mind.

Personal responsibility

We would like to blame our genes
  or poor environment,

---

* Isaiah 29:13

or inadequate education,
or social pressures,
or life's unfairness;

obviously,
it must be something to do with other people!

God has, however, given to each of us
the dignity and the privilege
of being responsible – and answerable –
for our own acts and attitudes.

It seems as if there is an evil twist within us;
but how we deal with it depends on us.

A plea for help
Lord,
you know us far better than we know ourselves.

You know how badly we react to criticism,
how quick we are to judge other people,
and even quicker to excuse ourselves;

we want to blame other people
for our mistakes and faults and frailty;

we close up our minds and hearts;
we cling to things that are not good for us.

Lord, help us;
we are trying to be honest with ourselves,
and with you;
help us to admit our faults
and confess our sins.

Show us what spoils us, imprisons us, enslaves us;
show us how we can be free within ourselves.

Lord, help us,
    have mercy on us;
    forgive us;
    and set us free from evil's power.

Mark 7:24-37
(Matthew 15:21-28)

For Jesus' encounter with the Gentile woman see page 51.

HELP MY UNBELIEF _____

It's good and right to see
    in more and more major Church assemblies
    a figure standing prominently at the front
    and 'signing'.

It's only right for those who are disadvantaged
    by being deaf and so perhaps not able to speak.

It's good for the rest of us to be reminded
    just how many of our sisters and brothers
    are so marginalised and excluded from so much.

Too often Christian worship concentrates
    only on singing hymns and hearing sermons;
    and if there is little to see or to do
    it is of little help for folk like these.

Two millennia later,
    with loops and ramps and other aids,
    we're catching up with our Lord at last.

He had no problem with communication.

Jesus was 'signing'

They brought this man to Jesus
   who took him away from the crowd
   so they would not see what he did
   and get the wrong impression.

All the extravagant gestures –
   touching the man's ears and tongue,
   Jesus' great exhalation of breath,
   with exaggerated movements of his own hands,
   and saying 'Ephphatha' in case the man could lip-read
   – all this was to help the man believe.

Suddenly he could hear and speak.

Keep it secret

Most times such healings were accompanied
   with an injunction to tell no one
   which seems quite pointless.

He did not say,
   'Don't tell them you can hear and speak',
   he said, 'Don't try to tell them how'.

'Do not say,
   "He just put his fingers in my ears and I could hear;
   he simply spat and sighed and touched my tongue
   and I could speak."

I don't have magic fingers or spittle or breath.
   It's faith that makes you whole.'

A boost to faith

Sometimes he touched the sufferer,
   sometimes a firm grasp, as with the leper,

most times his sure, strong word alone was needed;
always his method matched the need.

All these were intended to build up faith
just as he gives you bread and wine.

Lord, I have faith;
help me where faith falls short.

Mark 8:27-38

His confrontation with the would-be army of 5000 (page 45), his reappraisal of his work while roaming Gentile lands (page 50), and this vital conversation at Caesarea Philippi (page 53) proved to be a watershed in the ministry of Jesus.

LOVE AND SUFFERING _____

He came to love.

That was his essential mission –
    not to die,
    not to suffer,
    but to love;

    and if it should be
    that loving involved suffering,
    he would not stop loving.

In his necessary reappraisal
    he had confirmed this choice;
    however much it cost
    he would keep to the way of Love.

In the northern highlands
    he shared this commitment with his friends.

New teaching

From this point onwards
he worked mainly with the Twelve,

rather than with the crowds;

and he began to teach them
deeper truths than they had known before
– that God is Abba,
about prayer, and humility, and service,
and how the way of love may be the way of the cross.

But they were as resistant as we are
    clinging to old ingrained ideas.

Love and suffering

If you love someone
    you lay yourself wide open to being hurt:
    love and suffering are intermingled.

He was speaking to his disciples
    about suffering for the sake of the Kingdom
    but his insights are relevant to all our pain and hurt.

He, alone of all the world's great religious leaders,
    acknowledged the inescapable fact of suffering.

For others he confronted and challenged and healed it;
    for himself he would not avoid or evade it.

The suffering of Jesus

Watch how he dealt with it:
    'Keep your eyes on me,' he said.

When it became inevitable that he would die,
    he accepted it,
    still trusting the Father.

Somehow he seemed to absorb the suffering in himself.

We often make others suffer for our own hurt;
    find it hard to bear our pains
    and take it out on someone else;
    that's not the way of Jesus.

He held the pain within himself,
    stopped it going any further,
    and let the evil do no more harm.

He acknowledged, accepted, absorbed the suffering,
    transmuted and transformed it into a means of victory.

The way of Love
    may become the way of the cross
    but it is the way of Life.

See also 'Following can be costly', *Sunday by Sunday,* volume 1, pages 114-16.

Mark 9:30-37

Many scholars suggest that 9:37 and 10:15 were accidentally reversed at an earlier stage in the transmission of the gospel: 10:15 (becoming like a child) fits better with Jesus teaching the disciples about humility; 9:37 (receiving little children) seems better suited to follow 10:13-14. This meditation (and that of proper 22) assume this interchange.

THE CHILD IN THE MIDST _____

That autumn he did not know in detail
    what would happen the next Passover,
    any more than you can tell precisely
    what will happen to you in six months' time.

The Incarnation was that real.

He knew by then that it was possible,
    perhaps even probable,
    that he might suffer for what he said and did and was
    but he hoped not.

Who's in charge?
Although they did not, would not,
take seriously what he said,
    perhaps his repeated talk of dying had unnerved them
and turned their thoughts to what came next.

He had clearly said that Simon would be in charge
   – they had always assumed it would be Iscariot;
   and James and John were quite ambitious.

His disciples are still too concerned
   with priority, place, prestige, and power.

A new social order

A Jewish child had no legal standing;
   he (and even more, she) had duties but no rights,
   responsibilities but no privileges.

Jesus stood a child amidst the Twelve
   not with sentimental ideas of purity or innocence
   but as an example of total dependence.

He completely inverted the old social values:

   in the Kingdom of God
   the greatest is the least,
   the first is last,
   place and prestige count for nothing,
   and the essential characteristic is humility.

Two millennia later,
   we have not yet really taken that on board.

Becoming as a child

Are your eyes still wide with wonder
   to be in such a wonderful world?

Do you still expect miracles
   or has life become predictable and pedestrian,
   and no more than you expected?

Do you think that you know all you need to know
     or do you still want to learn?
If you are no longer learning you are not growing.

Do you realise you still need help to live well?

Being child-like does not mean being childish
     it means wanting to grow up.

Growing up
Do you really want to grow up –
     to the full-grown stature of a mature child of God?

When a fond relative asks a child,
     'What are you going to be when you grow up?'
     they really mean, 'What are you going to do?'

We are obsessed with 'doing' more than 'being'
     but what you are is more important than what you do.

A proper answer to that question
     would be, 'A woman' or, 'A man';
     the best answer is, 'To be like Jesus'.

You could be, you know.

All the above questions were provoked by 'The child in the midst' in
Cradle of Hope by the author.

Mark 9:38-50

THE FELLOWSHIP OF SALT _____

Embarrassed by his obvious criticism,
    they hurriedly changed the subject
    to divert the blame to someone else.

We all can be suspicious of other people
    whose ideas and attitudes are different from our own;
    despite better cooperation between the churches
    we still emphasise and exaggerate the differences.

Not only Jehovah's Witnesses think
    there will be no one else in heaven but them;

    sadly, some Christians are equally exclusive,
    think they have a proprietary hold on truth
    and reject all others who do not agree with them.

We have so much to share with other Christians

    and so much to learn from other faiths –
    if only we all had the prayer discipline of Muslims,
    the obedience of Jews,
    the sensitive spirituality of Hindus,
    and the Sikhs' calm acceptance of others.

Tolerance and acceptance is the key –
    to accept each other as Christ accepted us.

Amputation

However, Jesus used a graphic, brutal metaphor
  to emphasise that we must never ever tolerate
  anything that undermines another's faith.

Our own faith may even need such amputation –
  it is worth any sacrifice to enter the kingdom.

Is there anything you have to give up
  for the sake of the Kingdom,
  for the sake of unity,
  for the sake of your brothers,
  for the sake of your Lord?

Saltness

A church that's worth its salt *
  has truth to preserve, healing to channel,
  and offers light and life;

  but if it is not enlivening, or enlightening,
  healing people, preserving truth,
  it is not really a church –
  a holy club, a friendly institute, a caring society perhaps,
  but not a church.

The fellowship of salt

The apostles' bitter unforgiving of Judas
  began in hurt and anger
  because he had broken bread with them
  and then betrayed them.

* See also *Sunday by Sunday*, volume 1, page 66.

There is salt in bread
and sharing salt was a sacred vow of loving allegiance,
like blood-brotherhood with American Indians
and Christians at the Eucharist.

It meant being ready to do anything for each other,
to make any sacrifice for your brother,
to go to any lengths for him,
to give your life if need be.

Mark 10:2-16 (see also 9:37)

CHURCH AND CHILDREN ─────

Many churches now have very few children;
    there are even some where children are not wanted;
    but children are very precious:
    do not forbid them.

People say they are tomorrow's Church
    but our children are much more than that –
    they are a vital part of the Church of today,
    as important as the most senior and most respected member.

Of course they will disrupt our peace and quiet,
    but they have important things to teach us.

They are not Victorian children
    and if they are not heard,
    they will not be seen for long.

A child challenges the Church
It's so very different now from when I was a child.

I learned so much Scripture in day school;
    now they learn little if any.

Charles Wesley was right –
    we learn the faith from the hymns we sing:

I sang at least 15 every Sunday;
now our children may sing no more than two –
and they are not the 'great hymns of the faith' –
little solid faith is imbibed subconsciously.

The Sunday School movement
has served the Church well for a century
but now is in decline.

That's the pressing challenge:

how do we teach the faith
to the few children we have?

And how do we increase the few?

Parents and children

Once again, some Pharisees were trying to trap Jesus
and perhaps get him to contradict himself. *

Then, as now, the matter of divorce
was a contentious question.

Mosaic law allowed some to divorce; †
Mark, here, extended Jewish law
to permit a woman to sue her husband,
following Roman practice;
because some Christians were finding this too rigorous,
Matthew extended the exceptions. ‡

Jesus went back beyond the commands of Moses
to what God intended,
to what we were made for.

* Matthew 5:31 † Deuteronomy 24:1 ‡ Matthew 5:32

He saw the two sexes on absolutely equal terms
  and marriage as the holiest personal relationship.

Later, in conversation with the Twelve,
  he took that ultimate ideal to its logical conclusion.

With an almost equality of sexes,
  changing perceptions of partners' roles
  and the continued changing of the marriage institution;
  with *carpe diem* and *laissez-faire*,
  and liberty becoming licence,
  human relationships are not always ideal.

Confronted with an estranged couple,
  we, like Jesus, must insist on doing the most loving thing
  for all involved;

  and if all involved
  includes one, or 2.4, or any number of children,
  they must have priority;
  too many human casualties are growing up around us.

With all respect to the costly faithfulness of single parents,
  it still would seem that children benefit most
  within a good and wholesome marriage.

Church and children
Still most parents bring their child to church
  to be blessed by Christ and 'christened';

  we welcome them all,
  and dare forbid none;
  and we celebrate God's prevenient grace
  as we welcome them
  and mark them out for Christ.

Most significantly, in many churches,
   the *first* promise that is made
   for the care and nurture and loving of that child
   is made not by the parents,
   nor by the god-parents or sponsors,
   but by the Church.

Mark 10:17-31

Matthew alone says that the man was young. Luke says he was a 'ruler', which implies he had responsibility for others – and that puts a different 'spin' on what Jesus demanded.

JUST PLAIN SELFISH? _____

Why did Jesus quote only six Commandments?
And why did he put them in the wrong order?

All the Commandments which Jesus quoted
    are about relationships with other people.

Was this man pious, God-fearing, devout,
        and sincerely seeking the Kingdom,
        but had problems relating his religion to other people?

Why did Jesus change 'covet' to 'defraud'?
Did he know something we are not told?

Is the Commandment about 'honouring your parents'
    put last to emphasise it?

Was this a man of humble origins
    who had bettered himself
    and was now ashamed of his roots?

Was he ashamed of his parents?
Might he have used the law of Korban *

* See Matthew 15:5.

to deny them the help
which they might have naturally expected?

But if he was essentially selfish
why did Jesus warm to his earnest sincerity?

The danger of possessions

Jesus was always wary of possessions
and told many cautionary tales
– the best-known is this one about the camel.

They laughed at the impossible picture he painted
of the largest animal they knew
struggling to get through the smallest hole they knew,
which was the eye of a needle.

There was, in fact, no narrow gate into Jerusalem
where a camel had to be unloaded to get through
but the point was well made.

There are things we may need to 'unpack'
if we are to enter the Kingdom.

We are as acquisitive as jackdaws,
may even be jealous of those with more than us,
and it seems the more we have the more we want.

After a generation of serving Mammon,
we are finding a deep spiritual need
that is not satisfied by what we own.

Jesus was quite sure –
it is quite impossible
for God to rule in the heart of a man
who has too many possessions.

A deeper commitment
This man was challenged to give away his possessions
  because they mattered too much to him.

What gets in the way of our deeper commitment
  as individuals,
  or as a Church?

There are so many ways
  to keep God at arm's length,
  so he can't get through to us
  and we can't grow.

And it's not only about possessions.

Poverty may be just as much a barrier,
  so may resentment,
  or jealousy,
  or refusing to forgive;

  fear of change can keep God at a distance,
  so can fear of the unknown,
  or fear of being hurt,
  or self-pity,
  or self-satisfaction.

What is he asking you to give up
  or to let go of?

Mark 10:35-45

In Mark's gospel, every prediction of the Passion is followed by a negative response from his disciples which shows how little they understand.

THE SERVANT KING _____

He will not sign blank cheques.

He will give you all that you need
    and much more beside,
      often more than you have expected,
      always much more than you realise.

But he will not give you everything you want
    nor everything you ask for.

What you ask might not be his to give;
    it might be neither good nor right for you,
    or for him.

Whether it was James and John themselves
    or their mother who interceded for them
    matters little;

    and the indignation of the other ten
    makes it clear they were no better.

How little they realised or would accept
    that the Kingdom is about service,
    its insignia a manger, a towel and basin, and a cross.

Baptism and cup

He was speaking of the cup of suffering,
    the cup from which he shrank in dark Gethsemane.

The disciples' glib and quick reply to his question
    shows how little they understood his way
    or had counted the cost of following;
    they were so concerned with privilege and status.

And when this King was lifted up
    and made the cross into his throne
    from which he rules the world
    see who is on his right hand and his left!

Remember
    you too have been baptised into his way
    and share his cup at every Communion.

Being his disciple means
    that you also share the fellowship of his sufferings

    and you cannot be glib or blasé about that. *

A ransom for many

The Fathers of the early Church
    wrestled with this great saying,
    trying to decide to whom the ransom was paid.

It could not be to God if he is as Jesus teaches;
    but are we all in thrall to evil?

One of many convoluted explanations
    even saw Jesus as the cheese in a celestial mousetrap
    to trick and trap the Devil!

* See *Sunday by Sunday,* volume 1, pages 186-87.

Such questions are about as profitable
    as working out how many angels fit on a pin-head
    and they belittle what, by his suffering,
    Jesus has achieved for you.

The key-words are
    ransom, redeem, save, deliver, liberate.

At the foot of the cross
    you may realise but a fraction of the cost

    and can find that he liberates you
    from the sins that hold you back,
    the things that spoil you;

    he delivers you from your inner chains,
    saves you from being hostage to fortune
    and sets you free to love.

Mark 10:46-52

Mark positioned this story very carefully – there was still so much that his disciples could not see or understand.

ONE IN A CROWD _____

Looking in wonder at the sky at night
　　or standing in awe at the foot of a mountain
　　you may feel quite insignificant;

　　and mingling with a crowd
　　you may feel quite unimportant:
　　if you were suddenly plucked away
　　most would not notice;

　　everyone is so busy
　　and involved with their own problems
　　it can seem that your needs
　　matter little to anyone else.

So it must have been for Bartimaeus,
　　and the response of those around him
　　confirmed the insignificance he felt.

It was festival time,
　　with thousands going to Jerusalem,
　　among them many who hoped to see this preacher;
　　and the shouting of the beggar by the roadside
　　made it hard to overhear the rabbi's words
　　for he was teaching as he travelled.

Take heart

There is always one
   who has time for you,
   who has help for you,
   who is always ready to wait and listen.

Your voice is not lost among so many others,
   even in the great cacophony of mingled cries,
   he hears every whispered call for help.

He is not like a human switchboard,
   taking only one call at a time;
   nor will he put you on hold,
   and play frustrating celestial music while you wait!

He is always ready to wait and listen,
   always ready to help and heal.

Coming to him

Like Bartimaeus
   we must be persistent in our prayers;

   respond promptly to his calling us,
   not wait to marry, bury a relative, or buy a new car;

   we must rid ourselves of everything that hinders us,
   every sin that can hold us back.*

I want my sight back

I do not ask for 'the blessedness of when I first believed':
   there was joy in those halcyon days of first faith
   but I do not want to go back there.

---

* See Hebrews 12:1

Nor does getting my sight back
    mean 'wishing I was 25 again, knowing what I know now',
    for the whole point of being 25
    is that I didn't know then what I have learned since.

I would like to be able to see again
    as once I could with the wondering eyes of a child.

But if I am to follow Jesus
    I need to be able to see him more clearly,
    where he is going, what he is doing.

John 11:32-44

WHY DOES HE NOT COME? _____

Lazarus was dying
   but Jesus did not come.

Martha was getting quite distraught,
   trying to keep busy to hide her frustration:
   why did he not come?

'But it would be so dangerous for him,'
   Mary answered quietly,
   looking up from her prayers.

But Martha kept looking down the road –
   why did he not come?

It is a familiar cry.

From Hezekiah's Jerusalem under siege,
   from beside the waters of Babylon,
   from under the oppressive heel of Persians,
   and then of Greeks, and then of Romans,
   age after age, the self-same cry:
   why does he not come?

Then the young Church, looking for his Return,
   as days became weeks became months became years:
   why does he not come?

Today, after so many years of waiting,
 some have almost given up hope;

 people viciously oppressed, longing for deliverance,
 those suffering from terminal disease, aching to die,
 begin to wonder if he will ever come.

His ways are not our ways;
 his purposes are far beyond our small understanding;
 what seems good to us is seldom for the very best.

He still cares,
 still holds us in his heart, as he held Lazarus,
 and, when the time is right, he will come.

We need to learn and emulate his patience.

When he came
The story of Jesus raising Lazarus is a sign.

Christ is Lord of life,
 and Conqueror of death;
 and the new life which he brings
 is offered here and now
 as well as hereafter.

In Dorothy Sayers' *The man born to be king*,
 someone asks the resuscitated Lazarus at a celebration
 what it is like beyond death;
 he says nothing about long tunnels or distant light
 but talks of a man weaving a carpet.

Watching someone knit a fair isle jumper is the same:
 from one side it all looks such a mess,
 a tangle of unrelated threads and colours;

but seen from the other side
the most wonderful and intricate patterns are revealed.

So God is interweaving every action and accident,
 bending and turning every unruly deed,
 all into one breathtaking pattern
 that fits his own sublime, eternal purpose.

All Saints' Day
What has this lection to do with all the saints?

It may be that Lazarus, dead and buried,
 is a reminder of those whom St Paul believed
 are sleeping until Christ calls them forth
 when the last trumpet sounds.

Today, we honour and thank God,
 not only for Mary, Martha and Lazarus,
 but for all the friends of Jesus
 who have faithfully lived and died.

Many, like Mary, have listened to his voice,
 have been sensitive to him, shared his sorrows,
 and patiently prayed.

Others, like Martha, have protested at injustice,
 and given him practical, down-to-earth obedience,
 serving him in his impoverished sisters and brothers.

All, like Lazarus, have responded to his call,
 have caught a glimpse of the eternal,
 and found new life in Christ.

So also we, who want to be his friends,
 may find a new quality of life here and now
 as well as at the end.

We too need to respond when he calls our name,
    to serve him in ordinary ways,
    to pray patiently,
    and to keep trusting him.

Have faith and you will see the glory of God
    both here and hereafter.

See also 'Blessed by God' in *Sunday by Sunday*, volume 1, page 139.

Mark 12:28-34

HOW FAR IS NOT FAR? _____

On 24 May 1738,
  just before he went out,
  John Wesley opened his Bible at this text
  – and felt it spoke directly to him.

In fact, his Bible fell open at a well-thumbed page,
  a passage often yearned and prayed over;
  mine would open nowadays at John 2:10
  or 2 Corinthians 4:8;
  where would yours automatically fall open
  – or would it?

There are some folk who seem to think
  we can use the Bible like a magic box of messages,
  just letting it fall open and what you read
  is what the Spirit is saying to you today.

That could be very dangerous.
You can easily imagine some most inappropriate texts
  where you might accidentally land!

The Holy Spirit does not work that way.
The Bible is not a tool for any superstition or magic,
  but to be well-thumbed, prayed and yearned over.

How far is 'not far from the Kingdom'?

John the Baptist was not far away in time *
   but he was 'less than the least in the Kingdom'
   because he was so far off in understanding:
   he preached judgement but not mercy.

Judas Iscariot was not far from the Kingdom:
   but he was so sure he knew the better way
   and had not yet grasped the measure of Jesus' love.

This scribe heard how Jesus answered the Sadducees
   and very much approved;
   acknowledging the very heart of the Law,
   he needed only to obey it.

Definitions

We need carefully to define the proper love of self;

   we still need to define love for our neighbours –
   as much concern for their preservation and health
   as for our own,
   with as many allowances for their weaknesses and failures
   as for our own;

   love will have no better definition than Paul's. †

How?

Don't be put off
   because the love which Paul defines
   seems way beyond what you can manage.

---

* See *Sunday by Sunday*, volume 1, page 21. † 1 Corinthians 13:4-7

That great song of love
  describes how God loves you:
  his patience with you,
  and his kindness to you:

  he takes no offence in what you do,
  keeps no score of your wrongs,
  takes no pleasure in your sin.

There is nothing he will not face for you,
  no limit to his trust in you,
  no limit to his high hope for you;
  no limit to his love for you.

And when we can really see that
  the only proper response has to be in answering love
  and in asking his help to love others as he loves us.

Mark 12:38-44

MOTIVE MATTERS _____

It is not wrong
    to be respected by other people,
    or to be a prominent church leader,
    or to be on the top table at banquets;
    but is it deserved or sought?

The BBC once insisted that any prayer (at 9.55)
    needed no more than 17 words;
    but I have known some interminable vestry prayers,
    embracing every universal need
    and threatening a prompt start to public worship!

Jesus was not condemning all long public prayers as such,
    nor clergy wearing cassocks,
    but the searching question was
    why they did such things.

He could see some scribes,
    striding pompously about,
    looking even more smug than usual
    because he had approved of the scribe
    who was 'not far from the Kingdom' *

* See Mark 12:34.

They were so full of their own imagined importance
and so clearly wanted to impress people.

Were their long prayers to men or God,
intended to help people or for prestige?

He had to condemn such arrogance
and warn his disciples against conceit or every kind.

Don't seek power, prestige, or reputation.

Religion is not for what you get out of it.

Comes a widow
Some of those strutting scribes were rich Sadducees.

It was well within the Law, and not deliberately cruel,
to buy up the property of helpless widows:
but was their main concern for their own profits?

Such fat-cats made great show of what they gave,
and made sure that they had plenty left;
but she, who may have been robbed by one of them,
gave all she had.

How much to give?
It seemed only a pittance
but the value is always relative.

Christian giving has to be proportional.

I have known Christian stewardship pledges
of £5 which could well have been £20
and of £6 which should have been only £2.

The first time I heard of a 'Lord's jar'
    was when an underpaid lorry driver,
      delighted to bring £200 to an appeal for famine relief,
    told me about that special jar
    and about tithing every pay-day.

Is your own Christian giving
    a proper proportion and realistic?

This widow had very little
    but, like the lad with the loaves and fishes, *
    she gave all she had.

* See also page 126.

Mark 13:1-8

Mark's 'little Apocalypse' is very different in style from the rest of his Gospel. Written after the experience of famine, earthquake, volcano, and fierce persecution, all three synoptic gospels record this apocalyptic prophecy on Olivet.

THE END OF THE WORLD _____

One man confidently announced
    that the world would end in August 1948
    and it did – for him!

From time to time,
    someone, not understanding the book of Revelation,
    will also claim a special premonition,
    perhaps dash off to Egypt to measure the pyramids,
    then confidently announce the date of Armageddon.

Wiser soothsayers, like Nostradamus, suggest a date
    considerably beyond their expected life span.

Some people get totally obsessed
    with the prospect of the world's end;
    most others completely disregard it
    though many have some secret apprehension.

Apocalypse
Apocalyptic writing was especially popular
for a hundred years either side of Jesus.

Much, like the Book of Revelation,
    was written in a code which the readers knew,
    to encourage them in times of persecution or trouble,
    and seeming prophecies were fulfilled then.

St John's Antichrist was the Roman emperor,
    not Napoleon, Kaiser Bill, Hitler, Stalin,
    or any other megalomaniac.
Their terrors only confirm what Jesus said.

Jesus and the End
They had seen 'the Lord coming to his temple'
    which should inaugurate the day of judgement,
    so his first four disciples asked Jesus
    about his eschatology.

Warnings and a call to watchfulness
    run throughout this collection of his sayings.

He could see quite clearly
    that violent nationalism could only have one end
    and it was not far off.

He had always rebuked those who wanted signs;
    there would be inevitable wars and rumours of wars
    but they are not signs of the End;
    however, the End will certainly come.

If you're the kind of person
    who takes a premature look at how a novel ends,
    or takes a peep at crossword puzzle solutions,
    or wants to know everything,
    you'll just have to be patient!

No one knows the day or the hour.

Take no notice of the so-called signs
  they do not necessarily mean the end is near.

Be on your guard.

John 18:33-37

WHAT IS THE TRUTH? _____

What is the truth about Pilate?

Was he a capable and competent governor,
    or a weak and somewhat unimaginative civil servant,
    or a ruthless, hard, and decisive politician?

Bitter at being politically down-graded
    and posted to this unruly backwater of a province,
    he neither liked nor understood the Jews;
    their leaders had bettered him three times already,
    and he was wary of them.

He was irritated to be roused before dawn,
    and dragged outside to satisfy their religious quirks;
    and then he saw the prisoner.

The Kingdom

What is the truth about the Kingdom?

Pilate did not understand about a kingdom
    which claims and holds no territory
    and has no boundaries on a map.

He did not understand about a kingdom
which is not maintained by a ruthless army

and whose citizens would not fight,
even to defend their king.

He could not understand about a kingdom
where supreme authority did not depend on corruption,
and was not at risk from intrigue, murder, or coup d'etat.

The Kingdom of Christ is not of this world,
but is present in this world
whenever a man or woman opens their heart
to let God rule their life.

The Kingdom is not a place but an allegiance,
a relationship with God, who is Father and King,
to be trusted and obeyed.

The Kingdom is an unswerving commitment
to justice and compassion and peace,
to integrity and truth.

Pilate began to lose his way;
it is clear who was in chains.

Truth

What is the truth about Truth?

Truth is Truth is Truth
and is not bendable or cynically expendable.

Pilate was starting to panic;
every loop-hole he tried came to nothing;
the decision was his alone.

He could hear the open threats;
and his career was on the line.

Too weak or too cynical or afraid,
    he decided it was most expedient
    to compromise the Truth.

The King

What is the truth about this King?

He stood for compassion, understanding and integrity,
    for freedom, justice, and truth;
    he stood against all that Pilate stood for,
    and would not yield.

He was executed for treason,
    and in his dying witnessed to the eternal truth of love.

He is himself the Truth
    that is the way to life;
    and he must never be compromised by his servants.

There is no higher authority than Jesus;
    his Kingdom is an everlasting Kingdom.

He is the King of kings;
    not only can he be trusted,
    but he should be obeyed.

. . . continuing

YEAR C

THE YEAR OF THE SUFFERING SERVANT

THE GOSPEL ACCORDING TO LUKE

Luke 7:1-10

A MOST UNUSUAL MAN _____

The average centurion was a hard man,
  by reputation like a regimental sergeant major,
  needing to be strict and unbending,
  to control a hundred conscripted men.

This one was different.

It would have been quite normal
  for the centurion simply to let his servant die –
  slaves were expendable and easily replaced.

Such caring for a servant was quite rare.

Despite all their protests to the contrary
  too many of today's managers and employers
  have insufficient care for servants or employees:
  people matter more than efficiency or profit.

Most centurions, like most Roman officials,
  detested being posted to this provincial backwater.

The Jews were almost ungovernable
  with their strict laws, unusual customs,
  and strange religion.

This centurion had a different approach:
  he respected these foreigners' beliefs and customs,

and was so impressed by their religious fervour
that he encouraged it by building them a synagogue.

No wonder they respected him.

He was so sensitive to their laws
   that he understood it might be difficult
   for Jesus to enter a Gentile house.

Such tolerant care and sensitivity
   are essentials of the Kingdom
   which comprises 57 varieties of Christian;
   and perhaps even many religions.

Faith is more than belief
Most of all this man had faith in Jesus.

Belief is very important,
   for what you really believe
   shows in what you are and do;
   but it is not faith.

We need to search out truth,
   question, quarry, dig out, delve for truth;
   intellectual assent is important
   but it is not healing faith.

Your wholeness does not depend
   on whether you believe there was a six-day creation;
   your peace does not depend
   on what you believe about the virgin birth;
   your joy and strength do not depend
   on belief about a bodily resurrection of Jesus.

Belief is important but it is not faith.

Trust and obey
Faith is not what you believe
  but *who*.

This centurion had heard of Jesus;
  like you, he may not actually have seen him;

  but from what he had heard
  he was prepared to risk trusting him.

He understood about authority
  and he dared to accept the authority of Jesus;

  and act upon it.

Even at that distance
  because of the centurion's faith
  his servant was healed.

'You are my friends
  if you do what I tell you':

  call him Lord
  and do what he says –

  you can trust him.

Luke 7:11-17

Luke alone records this story about the death of another only child as if to reinforce the story of Jairus' daughter. It is all typical of Luke's concerns: poor as well as rich, a woman as well as a man, a Gentile as well as a Jew; and doctor Luke uses deliberate medical terminology in the way Jesus speaks to the corpse.

RESTORING LIFE _____

Jesus and his followers were climbing the rocky path
  to the fair city of Nain, set on the hill.

The funeral procession coming from the city
  was going to the cemetery about a mile away;
  that cemetery is still there today.

The death of a partner can be most distressing
  but to lose your child must be even worse;
  it must seem the times are out of joint
  and the generations gone awry;
  you would rather it had been you than her or him.

It was even harder for a widow in Palestine;
  as well as the grief and pain
  of losing her young and only son,
  this woman was facing utter destitution.

Then Jesus, very deeply moved, stepped in.

Ignoring the legal uncleanness of his action,
   he laid his hand upon the bier;

   he addressed the young man's corpse,
   as a doctor would speak to a patient;
   and the young man sat up.

It was all so reminiscent of Elijah,
   raising the widow's son at Zarephath; *
   and, for these folk, especially of Elisha,
   who had raised a dead boy at Shunem, †
   (Shunem was only four miles away).

The people could talk of little else,
   sure that God had visited them through Jesus.

Raising the dead

There are three different stories in the Gospels
   of Jesus restoring the dead to life –
   Jairus' little girl who died before he got there,
   this young man on his funeral journey,
   and Lazarus, who was already buried.

Some Christians believe it happened as it's written;
   others of equal faith look for other explanations.

Whether you think it's historically true or not
   is entirely up to you –
   as my old professor, T. W. Manson, used to say:
   'You pays your money, and you takes your choice'.

Either way, as always in the Gospels,
   the meaning matters most;
   and the meaning is most true.

* 1 Kings 17:22 † 1 Kings 4:35

God is not so far away from us
    that he is unmoved by human suffering,
    but comes alongside us in our need,
    and always brings new life.

He has no favourites of race or creed:
    young and old,
    rich and poor,
    women and men,
    all can find new life in him.

Jesus is Lord of life,
    and conqueror of death;
    he is always moved to help by people's sorrow;
    and is always bringing a new lease of life.

Widows do not have their dead restored to life,
    as did the widow in the story;
    but many have found a new quality of life
    as Christ comes to them, in their sadness,
    and kneels beside them, among the broken pieces.

He does not give your loved ones back to you;
    but he has held them through death into life,
    and will keep them safe for you,
    and for himself,
    and for all eternity.

Luke 7:36-8:3

HIS WAY OF LOOKING ⸺

I was taught to hate Germans and Japanese,
   much warned against Roman Catholics and blacks,
   and expected to be homophobic;

   such narrow-minded, blinkered prejudice
   can take some rooting out.

Jews were renowned for prejudice,
   dividing people into Jews and Gentiles;

   Greeks despised all who did not speak Greek
   as no better than sheep – (baa-baa-baa) barbarians;

   Many English people are just as arrogant –
   'All that spoils holidays abroad
   is that there are so many foreigners'!

We then make God in our image
   and think he shares our prejudice:

   but he loves those whom we don't like,
   and those of whom we disapprove,
   and all those who are different from us,
   just as much as he loves us.

Restricted vision
Simon was feeling very smug;

others must see how broadminded he must be
inviting this young rabble-rouser to his home.

A rich man's dinner was an 'open house'
and poor folk often drifted in for scraps,
so no one noticed the woman at first.

But when she made such an exhibition of herself;
it was obvious to Simon what she was.

It's so easy to be blinded to someone by one fault.

I remember a barrack-room lawyer
whom we all dreaded in church councils:
an awkward man and such a nuisance,
we were all relieved when he was not there;

and then one day by accident
I discovered that he was responsible, secretly,
for the most imaginative care and generosity . . .

Don't make rash judgements about people:
there is always more to them than you can see.

Prejudice such as Simon the Pharisee's
is narrow, blinkered, judgemental;
so very, very small-minded,
and wrong.

To see as Jesus sees
Simon thought, 'That woman is a sinner',
while Jesus was thinking, 'This sinner is a woman'.

Jesus can see so much more.

He saw through Simon
and warned him;
he looked with compassion at the woman.

He saw her clearly, and loved her,
   not for what she might become
   but just as she was.

We need to learn his way of looking,
   his perspective on other people.

The eyes of the forgiven

The woman's offering and her tears
   were not meant to earn forgiveness;
   this was a thank-offering
   for she had been forgiven already. *

She must have met Jesus before that evening,
   and found new hope in his compassion,
   regained her dignity and self-respect,
   and found new purpose and direction in his love.

Picture her kneeling at his feet,
   pouring out the best she had
   in gratitude for what he had done for her –

   that's what Christian worship at its best should be.

He knows you through and through,
   sees you as you are,
   and loves you.

He accepts you, just as you are,
   forgives you anything and everything,
   and sets you free.

You will be thanking him for that
   for ever.

* Verse 47.

Luke 8:26-39

The calming of the sea and of terrified disciples is followed by the calming of a demented man. Both Luke and Mark (5:1-20) record this encounter; Mark says the man came running.

EX-LEGIONARY APOSTLE _____

He had such wild and almost superhuman strength;
   today's diagnosis would be melancholic mania.

He lived amongst the tombs;
   sometimes they bound him and he broke the chains;
   sometimes he ran amok
   and people shut the doors and boarded up the windows;
   the only people he saw were running away.

One day, in a very severe attack,
   he came thundering down the road,
   shouting and foaming at the mouth,
   broken chains rattling,
   arms and legs flailing in all directions,
   a terrifying sight.

One solitary figure in white was standing there,
   not running away, just standing there waiting,
   patiently waiting.

Jesus will not run from any danger
   or turn away from anyone.

He waits patiently for you to come to him,
    waits to set you free from all that troubles you,
    and give you peace.

Exorcism

The exorcism follows the familiar pattern –
    the man knelt before Jesus:
    Jesus was stronger than his whole regiment of demons.

He needed some visible demonstration of his cure
    and when the pigs were stampeded by his cries
    Jesus said, 'There go your demons'.

There's an ironic twist in the story
    when the demons ask to enter the pigs
    and the pigs rush headlong into the sea;
    there was a popular superstition
    that the sea was the abode of condemned spirits.

The story contrasts the well-being of 'Legion'
    with that of the pigs and their owners;

    but the pigs' drowning raises some awkward questions:

    was it right to take the men's livelihood away?
    did the pigs matter more than the man?
    were the men more worried about the money
    than about the animals?

Is business profit and the economy
    more important than the well-being of animals?

The townspeople asked Jesus to leave,
    but were they afraid of such obvious divine power
    or of the threat to their businesses
    or because they didn't want to be disturbed?

It's very sad
    that the only time that he came to them
    they asked him to go away.

Gentile apostle

The man who had now come to him
    wanted to be an apostle
    and travel with Jesus and the Twelve.

But Jesus sent him home,
    the first apostle to the Gentiles.

This is the only time that anyone is commanded
    to tell others what God in Jesus has done for them.

Just as from Israel's earliest experience,
    deliverance always precedes commandment,
    so this healing comes before the commission;

    now that he has set you free
    and you are in your right mind:

    go and tell the others.

Luke 9:51-62

ON THE WAY _____

Ever since the reforms of Nehemiah
    when Manasseh built a rival temple on Mount Gerizim,
    Jews had despised Samaritans
    and Samaritans had scorned all Jews.

Luke is the only writer to relate this encounter
    which explains the nicknames of James and John.

Even if your friendly approach is rebuffed,
    or if your obvious need is unkindly spurned,
    even if you are abused or scorned,
    Jesus will not permit any vengeance.

When in extremes of suffering himself,
    he would not indulge in any retaliation

    nor will he tolerate it in you.

Hard sayings

Two men offered to be disciples
    and Jesus called another;
    but none of the three realised the cost.

These were crisis days for Jesus
    and he dared not settle anywhere.

It is pleasant to put down roots
    but he may ask you to move on.

We are not called to be commuters,
    travelling up and down the same familiar track
    until it becomes a rut;
    we are called to be pilgrims.

But not yet

It is possible this man's father had died that day
    but more likely that he was still alive.

The man was ready to accept the demands of Jesus
    but not just yet.

We all like to stay with familiar things
    and hold on to long-used traditions;
    we even cling to old hurts and resentments;
    often we're quite happy as we are;

    but he calls us to new ways.

Attainable objectives

Whether ploughing or driving
    or simply walking,
    you need to look where you're going;

    and both you as an individual and your church
    need to know where you're going.

Long distance walkers plan an overall route
    but often move by stages,
    from one landmark to another.

A church needs both to know where it's going
    and to move deliberately in that direction
    but by measured and attainable stages.

How to get there

The writer to the Hebrews (12:1)
    sets clear way marks for following Jesus.

What would you want to take with you
    if your home was on fire?

Carry only the essentials for this journey,
    'throw off every encumbrance'.

A man sat by Bethesda pool for so long
    that Jesus had to ask him,
    'Do you really want to get better?'
    – enough to do something about it?

'Throw off every besetting sin',
    anything that drags you down or back.

'And run (or walk) with resolution . . .'

In the first halcyon days of being his disciple
    the grass is green, the sky is blue,
    and there is a lightness in your step.

But soon the grass gets sparser,
    the sky gets paler,
    the air gets dry and hot;

    and much of the journey, following Jesus,
    may seem like trudging through a wilderness.

Just keep on going, with resolution,
    'your eyes fixed on Jesus',
    for where he is going is where you want to be.

Luke 10:1-11, 16-20

Luke is the only writer to record the mission of the Seventy-two. It is possible that this mission was overlooked by the others because the Twelve became so prominent in the Church. But Luke was himself a Gentile and was always eager to record the dealings of Jesus with non-Jews.

EVERYONE A MINISTER _____

Seventy-two is, according to Genesis, *
   the number of all the nations of the earth;
   according to Jewish tradition
   it took seventy-two translators
   exactly seventy-two days
   to translate Hebrew scriptures into Greek.

A discrepancy in ancient manuscripts
   between seventy-two and seventy
   emphasises that the number is symbolic;
   here it represents the world mission of the Church.

The Twelve were sent out in two's
   so that the message could reach more people
   – seven times as many as Jesus on his own.

This time the Seventy-two were sent ahead
   to the towns he himself would visit
   to prepare the people for his coming.

* Genesis 10

The commission which they were given
    is very similar to that given to the Twelve *
    but there were some differences in preparation.

The Twelve were called to be with Jesus
    and to learn from him as they travelled
    so that they could be sent on mission;
    the Seventy-two were not given such training.

Lay ministry

To me it seems the Twelve are like those nowadays
    who are called and tested and prepared
    for ordained ministry;

    the Seventy-two are more numerous than the Twelve,
    and receive less training,
    but like the Church's laity have the same commission.

For 40 years I struggled with
    'Leave it to the minister
    – he gets paid for it'!

But during those years,
    we have rediscovered what ministry is:

    we are all ministers, clerical and lay,
    all part of the ministry of the whole Church
    to the whole world.

If you have not been ordained priest or presbyter,
    if you do not wear a dog-collar,
    you are a minister just as much as I am.

* Matthew 10

The symbolic flames of Pentecost
   rested on each and everyone
   because each and every one of us
   has a part to play in the ministry of the Church;

     as a renowned churchman said to me
     on the day that I retired from active work,
     'You will be a minister till the day you die!'

Superannuated now, I am having to discover
   what ministering means I have to be and do today;
   and so must you.

Working with Christ

Wherever we are today
   we are all expected to minister there.

It may not be where you feel called to be,
   or even where you want to be,
   or where he intends you shall be one day,

     but wherever you are today
     he needs you to minister there.

You may be the only one of us there,
   you may have to represent all the rest of us;
   certainly you have to represent Christ,
   to be as Christ to those around you.

It can be daunting to stand alone
   and so he sent his disciples out in two's;

     and then at Easter
     he smiled his Spirit upon them.

Nor will you ever stand alone:
   there will always be two of you,
   Christ and you, you and him.

And if you let his Spirit work in you
   and fill you with his love,
   they will see Christ in you
   and he will minister to them through you.

Luke 10:25-37

NEIGHBOURLY LOVE _____

This familiar story is often misinterpreted
   as if it represents the whole of Christianity;
    but loving God is as important as loving your neighbour.

Defining 'neighbour'

Your neighbour is not only anyone who helps you
   but anyone you meet who is in need,

   anyone abused by others or afraid of being so,
   anyone who feels beaten,
   or passed by and neglected,
   anyone who feels half-dead.

   Your neighbour lives next-door,
   across the street, across the city,
   is in the next car or at the next desk,
   and, in this TV global village,
   is anyone you see who is in need.

Defining Love

When the priest and Levite ignored the injured man,
   it only confirmed what many of those listening
   thought of priests and Levites;

and let's have no excuses about purity for Temple service,
these two had finished their duty
and were going the wrong way.

They waited for the third who must come along –
a good old reliable Jewish working-man:

and when Jesus said he was a Samaritan
there was a gasp of shock and horror.

The prejudice was so deep
that even the good man who had asked the question
could not even bring himself to say the word 'Samaritan'
but muttered, 'The one who showed him kindness'.

Love has no prejudice
and does not discriminate in giving or receiving help.

It was not unknown for a decoy,
with a liberal scattering of first-century tomato ketchup,
to be lying by the roadside,
while robbers hid in the ditch across the road:

but Love is not afraid of danger or of taking risks.

It took some time (as well as oil and wine and clothes)
to bandage up the wounds,
but Love is caring.

To foot the bill and keep on caring,
though it may be needed for a long time,
can be very demanding and even wearying;
but Love does not give up.

Why attempt such loving?

Because any victim is Christ himself

and inasmuch as you do it to others,
you are doing it to him.

Defining love of self

To love yourself as you love your neighbour
　　means doing no more for yourself,
　　and making no more excuses for yourself,
　　than you would for any other.

It means taking proper care of your whole self
　　– soul as much as heart, mind as much as strength –
　　and making time to do it,
　　even if it is inconvenient to your set life-style.

The heart of Christian love
　　is to treat other people,
　　judge other people,
　　help other people,

　　not as you are treated or judged or helped,
　　but as you would like to be!

Why?
　　Because Christ is the victim
　　and inasmuch as you do it to others,
　　you are doing it to him.

Christ the Samaritan

Sometimes, of course,
　　you yourself feel bruised and beaten,
　　ill-used by other people,
　　or so tired you can go no further;

　　and then Christ comes to you,
　　to bind up your wounds,

and share your troubles,
and help you on the way

and however long it takes,
he will not give up on you.

Luke 10:38-42

BALANCING ACT ─────────────

One can't help feeling sorry for Martha;
   she seems to get such a rough deal.

Most of us know what it's like
   to feel quite distracted
   with so much to do
   and not enough time to do everything.

Perhaps she had not planned every detail
   or set herself attainable targets;
   she was trying to do too much,
   and was panicking,
   and so got things out of proportion;

   we may know that feeling too.

Many of us think that we too are the Marthas –
   well, somebody has to do the menial, practical things;
   we can't all just sit and think and discuss;
   it would be nice if we could
   but just look at that dust!

Jealous
Was Martha jealous of Mary
   and wished she too had time

to sit at Jesus' feet and drink in his every word?

Martha, fretting and fussing,
　　was irritated by Mary just sitting there
　　when there was so much to be done;

　　　if Mary had got off her backside and helped,
　　　they might both have been able to listen.

And when Jesus praised Mary –
　　that was just about the last straw!

There's always a tension between action and stillness,
　　between being and doing.

Some of us seem to think an overflowing diary
　　is proof of our effectiveness and our importance,
　　and shows how hard we work for the Kingdom;
　　but what we are is more important than what we do.

Jesus himself needed both stillness and action.

He needed both the understanding support of Mary
　　and the caring activity of Martha;

　　the risen Christ coming to the lakeside
　　needed both John standing, gazing, wondering
　　and Simon working strenuously in the boat. *

Most of us need to be
　　both Martha and Mary,
　　Simon and John.

We need a balance of stillness and action –
　　and advisedly the stillness comes first!

* See John 21.

Sensitivity

Martha was getting quite distracted,
  but was she also insensitive to Jesus?

It has been suggested
  she was so excited that Jesus was coming to them
  that she wanted to provide extra-special hospitality;
  but perhaps it was not what *he* wanted.

Tired from his long travelling towards Jerusalem,
  and the clamour and demands of the crowds,
  and aware of what was waiting at this journey's end,
  did he just want to relax with his friends
  in the peace and quiet of Bethany?

Mary, always sensitive to his moods,
  was trying to understand and share
  while Martha was preparing a spread,
  but a spread was the last thing he wanted!

Why do we always think
  that we know best what other people need?

Why do we presume to impose on them
  our own standards and our ways of helping?

Sensitivity, such as Mary's, is born in stillness.

Luke 11:1-13

HOW MUCH MORE _____

The houses of most artisans
   had only one room.

There was a raised platform at one end
   under which the fire had burned in daytime
   so it was still warm when the family went to bed.

They each wrapped themselves in the blanket,
   which by law was every Hebrew's birthright,
   and laid side by side upon the shelf,
   looking just like a row of sausage rolls!

All their domestic animals –
   chickens, a couple of goats, and perhaps a donkey –
   were brought inside at night
   and the door was shut.

Midnight caller

Giving hospitality was a sacred duty,
   so when Reuben's unexpected guest arrived,
   Reuben went for help to Nathan
   and received a most inhospitable reply:

   'Will you please stop hammering on the door
   and go away – you've woken the kids already!

   'I know we've got some of today's bread left
   but I'm not getting up.

'It's pitch black – it must be nearly midnight –
I'll probably slip off the shelf, fall over the pans,
rouse all the chickens, and stumble into the goat.
I'm not getting up. GO AWAY!'

But Reuben kept on knocking,
    knowing they had the bread he needed;
    and Nathan, not wanting to become a laughing-stock
    or regarded as uncaring by the whole village,
    got up to help.

If so irritated and reluctant a man
    will give help to someone in need,
    how much more readily will the Father . . .

Persistence

It's a parable about persistence.

So also are the sayings which Luke adds at the end,
    for the word Jesus actually used
    means, 'Keep on asking . . . seeking . . . knocking'.

It is *not* about persistent nattering,
    hammering on God's door,
    going on and on and on
    until you shame him into responding.

The Father knows what you need before you ask
    and does not need persuading or cajoling.

It's about persistent praying,
    day after day after day;
    coming to the Father daily
    to receive what he is waiting to give
    until you have received all.

Luke 12:13-21

WHAT WENT WRONG? _____

As soon as there is chance of an inheritance
    forgotten relatives emerge from the woodwork.

I've seen it too often;
    I almost wrote 'suffered' it too often
    but then I would be accepting the same values.

Jesus would work hard,
    and still is working, to reconcile divided brothers
    but not if they are divided over possessions.

He was very suspicious of possessions
    and what they can do to people;
    so often they bring out the worst in us.

So he told this warning story.

So much is right
It's not wrong to work hard
    or to make a profit
    or to save
    or to provide for a pension
    or to eat and drink and be merry.

Having an abundance of good things is not wrong:
    you don't need to feel guilty
        because you were born in the West's lap of luxury
        while so many of your brothers and sisters
        are in such great need.

Being successful at work is not wrong:
    you are given talents to use
    and to use them to the full;
        although you might ask yourself, 'At whose cost?'

You are expected to make a profit from you labour
    but what you do with the profit is important.

John Wesley strongly advocated
    that you should save all you can;
    although he was actually insisting
    that you spend no more than you need to.

Jesus told us to live one day at a time
    and not to worry about the future;
    but some provision for the future is right.

All this must mean that some insurance is right;
    although I wish the Church was more concerned
    about assurance than insurance.

A foolish man

Despite all those qualifications,
    if so much of what he did is right,
    what was wrong with the man in the parable?

It's not simply a cautionary tale about mortality
    to remind you that there are no pockets in shrouds
    and that you can't take your possessions with you.

The clue to what had gone wrong
   is in the last line of the story:
   who will get it now?

Was there no one to inherit all this wealth?

Had he worked so hard
   that he had no time for a family or for friends?

Had he cared more about his profits
   than about his relationships?

Had he worked hard to be a success,
   to make a profit and to save
   to the exclusion of everything else?

Meanings

Work hard
   but not at the expense of your relationships.

Use your talents to the full
   but do not exploit other people.

Enjoy your abundance
   but remember to share generously with those in need.

Save for a rainy day
   but not as if you are expecting another Flood.

People matter more than possessions.

Luke 12:32-40

WATCHING AND WELCOMING _____

This parable seems more suitable for Advent
   than for August and the height of summer
   but it's always important to be mindful
   of the coming of the Son of Man.

How often do you wonder
   if he will come today?

Hope and speculation about his imminent return
   was a prime concern for early Christians;
   though by the time that Luke was writing
   the delay had modified their expectation
   to 'the middle of the night or just before dawn'.

Still in every generation,
   there are some so obsessed with the prospect
   that they try to predict the end of the world;
   but even the famous Nostradamus got it wrong
   for no one knows the day or the hour. *

However, we must have learned in Advent
   that he is always coming
   whether we are ready or not. †

* See page 179. † See *Sunday by Sunday,* volume 1, page 15.

Therefore the question is not 'Will he come today?'
  but 'When and where and how will he come today?' –

  for he is sure to be coming
  and we need to be alert.

The Second Coming

The emphasis here is very different
  from the way I was first taught
  and since then have thought and feared.

So much teaching about the End of all things
  has Matthew's threatening stress on Judgement,
  denouncing our guilt and shame –
  a dreadful, awful day of wrath,
  when we shall all pay for our misdeeds,
  when one will be taken and another left.

But here the emphasis is on blessedness:
  the coming of the son of Man
  will mean happiness for his people.

He will reverse the roles,
  as in the upper room;

  the master becomes the servant;
  he girds his loins,
  rolls up his sleeves,
  and waits on his servants.

So, in every eucharist,
  he comes not to be served but to serve;
  he comes and waits on you
  and you will be blessed indeed
  if he finds you alert and welcoming.

Heart's desire

Jesus warned his disciples
 there was little point in taking their possessions
 on this now-critical journey to Jerusalem;
 far better to sell all and give the proceeds
 to those in greatest need.

Jesus' perceived principle that you get
 whatever you really set your heart on
 is equally true for good and bad.

If a man wants to be a millionaire,
 really wants it above all else,
 so much so that he does not care what it costs
 in work or health or relationships,
 in duplicity or corruption,
 regardless of any crime or sin it may involve,
 he will probably manage it.

Alternatively and much longer-lasting,
 Jesus promises that if you set your heart
 on the eternal treasures of the Kingdom –
 those indestructible qualities of patience and kindness,
 goodness, faithfulness, and gentleness,
 and all the fruits of the indwelling Spirit –
 the Father will give them to you.

When he comes today,
 or when your days are over,
 or at the very end of Time,
 there is nothing to fear.

Make his Kingdom your heart's desire,
 whatever the cost;
 watch for him,
 work for him,
 and you will be blessed indeed.

Luke 12:49-56

TIME TO CHOOSE ─────────────

In parallel sayings, typical of Hebrew poetry,
   Jesus made yet another prediction of his Passion.

He had hoped for a ready response to his Good News,
   a nationwide repentance and turning to God;
   but so many were opposed to him.

A terrible ordeal loomed before him:
   he could see himself totally immersed in suffering,
   submerged under the weight of it;
   how he wished it was all over!

The fire he lit would set the world ablaze
   with new ideals, new visions, and new hopes;
   but it would bring desolation upon himself.

Fire, in Scripture, is normally a sign of judgement;
   and although unwelcome, warning of coming judgement
   was a persistent element in the teaching of Jesus.

His cross stands as a sign of judgement on the world.

Choosing

Jesus had refused to be divider between brothers
   but his trying to rouse people from their complacency
   would provoke and force division.

They would divide themselves
  and bring judgement on themselves.

Perennially, the old are critical of the young,
  while the young grow impatient with the old;
  Matthew expected such a clash between generations;
  but in Luke the division is within the generation
  and that is far more serious.

Choosing

All the people would have to choose –
  including those closest to Jesus.

Judas did, and the fleeing ten,
  and Simon, till even his strong nerve broke;

  Caiaphas and the Sanhedrin,
  and Pontius Pilate, all made their choice;

  at the centre of it all,
  Jesus himself could choose and did.

The decision was critical for them,
  especially at the turning of the times.

With hindsight of his death and resurrection,
  it is easier for us than it was for them
  but we too must decide –

  between the ways of Judas or Caiaphas or Jesus;
  self-will, self-interest or the way of love.

The cross stands in judgement on our choosing.

Signs of the times

English people talk so much about the weather!

Islands as small as ours, in this part of the globe,
are bound to enjoy (or not) frequent climatic variations.

Weather forecasts were more predictable in Palestine:
a sirocco wind from the desert would bring a heatwave;
clouds over the Mediterranean would bring rain.

They had learned that from experience;
but they could not read the signs of their moral climate,
nor see the moral and spiritual storm that was blowing up.

Are we any more perceptive than they were?

How do you read the signs of our times?
How do you assess the moral and spiritual climate?

Leading clerics regularly anticipate Revival – do you?

In 1950 W. E. Sangster gave ten good reasons
why we needed a religious revival;
but it did not come.

A hungry generation turned to the institutional Church;
we were found lacking;
and church attendances continue to decline.

On the other hand,
some young Christians are very confident and excited
about the future of the Church,
although they expect it to be very different
from what it is today.

The cross stands as a sign of judgement
on the choosing of this generation
and on the choosing of the Church
which will decide its future.

Luke 13:10-17

STAND TALL ⎯⎯⎯⎯⎯⎯⎯⎯⎯⎯

She had shuffled into the synagogue,
   so bent by spondylitis,
    that she looked as if she carried a heavy burden,
    or was like a slave under the yoke of oppression.

She did not ask for help,
   nor did she need to;
   he knows your need before you ask.

Jesus, mid-sermon, saw her,
   called to her immediately;
   stretched out his strong hands,
   and lifted her burden;

   and she stood tall and straight,
   her human dignity restored,
   and could look him in the eye.

He does not remove all burdens;
   he will always remove the weight of sin and guilt;

   you may have burdens which he will not lift,
   but he will certainly give you
   the strength you need to carry them.

He calls you to wholeness,
to raise your head and stand tall for the Kingdom;
and at the last to look him in the eye.

People more than rules
This synagogue must have been quite liberal
    to welcome Jesus so far on in his ministry,
    when most synagogues were closed to him;
    but the Pharisees were closely watching him.

Offended by this diversion with the woman,
    the president firmly rebuked Jesus –
    but not directly to his face;

        he used the well-known ploy
        of attacking one person through a general comment,
        a palpable device never to be used by preachers.

Jesus treasured Mosaic Law as much as any other,
    and would observe every jot and tittle,
    but never at the expense of other people.

Help and healing must never be delayed;
    today, and not tomorrow, is the day of salvation.

He echoed Amos and the prophets
    in his attack on the hypocrisy and sham
    of empty or shallow religion.

Still he challenges both society and the Church
    on the way we treat offenders or nonconformists;

        rules are essential
        but can be no more than guidelines,
        for there are always exceptions
        and we must never sacrifice people for principle.

Jewish Law preserved the rights of animals;
    man is appointed to master creation
    and to care for all its creatures
    until the wolf lies down with the lamb;

and people matter even more than animals.

Doctor Luke

Luke is the only evangelist to record this story;

> his early medical training
> (before he met Paul and became a Christian)
> gave him an understandable interest
> in the healing work of Jesus;
> many healing stories are unique to Luke's gospel.

Different people are drawn to Jesus
> by different aspects of what he is;
> what attracted Luke was very different
> from what drew the other evangelists.

As for me, I was first attracted
> by some of what Mark saw in Jesus
> and by much of what held Luke;

> it depends on one's own personality,
> one's own experience, hope, and need.

Always there is something about Jesus
> that speaks to you, rings bells for you,
> answers your hopes, and meets your needs.

And it changes –
> what drew me at 18
> is not what inspired me at 30,
> or held me at 45,
> or sustains me now.

There is always more to see in Christ
> than you have dreamed of.

Luke 14:1, 7-14

AFTER-DINNER SPEECH _____

The Roman world utterly despised
    the new Christian virtues of humility and gentleness.

They regarded meekness as weakness,
    and an Empire is not established or maintained
    by being weak;
    you have to be strong, and determined,
    and assert yourself.

The need to be more self-assertive
    is very much in vogue in our society today,
    and highly recommended if you want to get on.

(Strange how that verb seldom has an object –
    I always want to ask, 'Get on what?')

Imagine the conversation round the dinner table
    at the end of a two-day course on self-assertiveness!

Parables
Jesus had been invited to a Pharisee's house –
    it gave them a chance to see him at close range;
    and they had laid a trap for him with a dropsical man.

Then, as now, some hoped to use the occasion
    to their own advantage.

In the Church, as in the world,
    there are always some who want the best seats:
    James and John and the others were no exception.

Then, as now, there were always some
    who wanted to show off their imagined importance
    or to be seen with distinguished people,
    or to cultivate useful social or business contacts.

Jesus had to warn them
    that self-assertive pride and overweening ambition
    may be exposed to their own embarrassment,
    and have no place in the Kingdom.

What you are matters more
    than who you know or the company you keep.

The etiquette of the Kingdom
He developed the theme to include hospitality.

The list of guests which Jesus recommended
    is repeated in the parable which follows; *
    worldly considerations are superseded
    at the great feast of the Kingdom:
    Gentiles and outcasts are especially welcome.

If you are having a special celebration,
    of course you will want to invite
    your family and your closest friends.

When someone has entertained you to a meal,
    you will want to return the invitation sometime,
    or may feel under an obligation to do so.

* Luke 14:15-24

That's the point of Jesus' guest list:
    it's about repayment.

It was a cardinal article of Pharisees' teaching
    that they would be repaid for generous acts of charity
    at the resurrection of the just.

Such systems of rewards and punishments
    or the accruing of personal merits are of no account
    in the economics of the Kingdom.

Other people must always have priority
    and Christian giving expects nothing in return.

The pattern always is Jesus,
    who took an apron, a towel and a basin,
    and made himself a servant;

Jesus, who humbled himself,
    emptied himself of all but love,
    and gave himself to us,
    and for us.

Luke 14:25-33

Most modern translations (such as REB and Jerusalem) hold to the literal word which Jesus used and Luke recorded in verse 26, although others (such as GN) paraphrase the meaning, as below.

FOREWARNED IS FOREARMED _____

He didn't tell his disciples at first,
    not to beguile them into following him,
    nor to conceal the truth and soften the blow,
    but because he did not know.

As soon as he realised
    how hard the way of love would become,
    he shared it with them.

They were his friends
    and he would not leave them in the dark.

Jesus would never ask that they hated anyone;
    the strong Semitic word exaggerated his point.

In the crisis he was facing
    he needed them to give him absolute priority,
    to 'love their dearest less' than they loved him.

He certainly did not exaggerate about the cross;
    they might have to die for him and for the Kingdom.

Being prepared

Luke alone added the vivid pictures
  of the king and the would-be tower builder.

Jesus, preparing for the approaching battle,
  needed to be as sure of his small band of friends
  as Gideon had been of his tiny army. *

The broken-down stump of an unfinished watchtower
  in the ravaged remains of a vineyard
  would make the builder a laughing stock
  and be a lasting monument to his folly.

The need to watch was a familiar injunction;
  a vineyard watchtower was significant for Israel.

These simple parables were well chosen:

  Don't start what you cannot finish;
  don't come with me if you're not prepared to die:
  to die for me,
  or to self,
  or both.

Self-sacrifice

For them it meant being ready to die for him;
  for us it means being ready to live for him
  and will always involve self-sacrifice.

By now, you probably have little money left
  through your generous response to his call
  to give to those in need;
  but that's the least of what it costs.

* Judges 7:7

There's also the wear and tear of loving,
 forgiving the deepest hurts and keeping on forgiving,
 the hurt of being taken for granted,
 of being misrepresented or misunderstood,
 of being ridiculed and thought foolish
 by those who don't share your vision or commitment.

There's the cost of keeping faithful,
 even when you don't feel like it.

Despite his repeated warnings,
 some of us may not have calculated the cost
 when he first called us to follow him.

By the time we understood more clearly,
 for us, as for the Twelve, it was too late to give up;
 he meant too much to us by then;
 who else could we go to?

All the resources of his love,
 which are at your disposal,
 will never be expended.

He will not stop building you up in faith and love
 until the work is completed
 and you have become what you are meant to be.

He will battle for you and with you
 till the victory is won.

You will never be defeated.

See also 'Following can be costly', page 56 and 'Love and suffering', page 147; 'salt' sayings feature on pages 153 and 154.

Luke 15:1-10

Two parables from everyday experience prepare Jesus' hearers for the message of the third parable (15:11-32) which again ends with a banquet. Matthew (18:12) applied the first to lapsed Christians but Luke was most concerned with outcast sinners.

LOST AND FOUND ──────────────

Jesus addressed most of his parables to Pharisees,
    never needing to justify his actions,
    but to keep his dialogue with them open,
    to explain his vision of the Kingdom
    and the truth about the Father.

Pharisees judged Jesus by the company he kept
    and accused him of condoning immorality,
    but the 'people of the land' who flocked to hear him
    knew exactly what he stood for.

Like the elder son in the next parable, *
    the Pharisees were, quite frankly, jealous
    of the welcome Jesus gave and promised
    to people whey did not like, accept, or understand.

Be careful of any rash judgements you may make
    about people you don't like or understand

* See *Sunday by Sunday*, volume 1, page 137.

whose standards and way of life
may be very different from your own.

Never envy a libertine's deathbed repentance,
implying he's got the best of both worlds;
if you have been found and shepherded by Christ
you undoubtedly have the best of this one
as well as of the next.

A wandering sheep
Many a village was a farming cooperative,
perhaps a forerunner of a kibbutz;
it may be that these villagers could afford
no more than a hundred sheep,
which were shepherded by a team of two or three.

Sheep are not as silly as they are supposed to be –
I saw one 'stupidly' sitting down on very frozen grass
and then get up to eat the breakfast she had thawed!

However, sheep are most likely to go wandering off,
as one of this flock had done and got lost;
a shepherd went off to find her.

Being a shepherd was hard and dangerous work,
risking life and limb, so often in the dark,
tracking and searching barren moorland
until he found the sheep –
or brought back a bloodstained fleece.

'What about the ninety-nine?'
a petulant church steward once asked me,
making the same mistake as the Pharisees.

The sheep had just been counted in
and the others were safe in the fold for the night
under the watchful eye of a fellow shepherd.

Imagine the joy and relief in the village,
   and for their tight economy,
   to see their friend bringing the lost one back.

Abraham and many of his descendants were shepherds;
   many of Israel's leaders and prophets
   had been shepherds.

Jesus too regarded the shepherd
   as a true picture of God
   and as a model for himself. *

Seeking the lost
A silver piece was more than one day's wage
   and most villagers were so very poor –
   a lost coin might mean no food for her family that day;
   one of ten pieces sounds very much,
   as if it came from her marriage headband –
   its loss as upsetting as if you lost your wedding ring.

No wonder she was desperate
   and told her nearest neighbours.

Her house was quite dark, with only one small window,
   and searching the rushes on the floor of beaten earth
   was like looking for a needle in a haystack.

It was such a relief when she found it
   and those who shared her concern also shared her joy.

The sheep had wandered away by itself;
   the coin was lost through the carelessness of someone else.

* See *Sunday by Sunday*, volume 1, page 179.

These parables have one simple, central meaning –
    of great joy in heaven when the lost are found.

Jesus astounded his critics and thrilled his friends
    with this new and original teaching:
    that God goes seeking the lost.

This is the prevenient grace
    which we celebrate when we baptise infants –
    long before they can know or understand,
    God loves them, seeks them, and receives them.

If you wander off, he'll come looking;
    when he finds you, there'll be great celebration.

Luke 16:1-13

BUYING FAVOURS

Jesus was not commending fraud;
    he applauded this steward
    because he acted cleverly,
    not because he acted dishonestly.

The parable has one simple meaning:
    show kindness to others
    and it could turn out to your advantage.

It raises important questions
    about money and friendship and stewardship.

Money

People still seem to think money can buy anything,
    that everything has its price,
    and that we must always have an eye
    on claiming compensation!

Compassion and justice seem to be brushed aside:
    Mammon rules – and it's not OK.

Adelaide Proctor wrote,
    'We have enough, yet not too much
    to long for more.'

Perhaps we have too much,
   and yet still we long for more . . .

and so we are still yearning for a deeper peace.

Stewardship

Paul did not say that money is the root of all evil; *
   it is neither good nor bad in itself;
   what counts is what you do with it.

This parable raises the nagging question:
   'Are you a reliable steward
   of what has been entrusted to you?'

'Produce your accounts;
   give an account of your stewardship',
   is addressed to each one of us
   and to all of us together in the Church.

Sometimes Christians together are found to be
   inept and inefficient and ineffective;
   no wonder he wished his people would use their wits,
   and suggested we should 'learn from the worldly'.

There is much that the Church could learn
   from the worlds of industry and commerce;
   but be careful –
   our aims and objectives are very different from theirs.

Money and friendship

This rogue of a steward panicked
   and decided friends are more important than money.

* 1 Timothy 6:10

Money can't buy friendship
  although many lottery winners suddenly discover
  they have far more friends then they had realised.

He decided that helping his master's debtors
  would at least put them under an obligation to himself.

He 'made friends' by writing off their debt;
  his action recalls the ancient Hebrew law of Jubilee *

  which inspired Jubilee 2000,
  the campaign to cancel the crippling debts
  that bedevil(led) so many developing nations.

This country has a poor record in Overseas Aid –
  we have never yet reached the target we accepted
  and we dare to attach trading-strings to what we give.

No wonder we are not regarded
  as very good friends by the poorest people.

Friends are so important
The galloping spread of the communication revolution
  may mean that people increasingly work at home,
  do their shopping from home,
  and communicate with friends, both near and far,
  from the comfort of their own armchair.

If they seldom 'see each other's face' †
  a church may well become one of the few places
  where the warmth of true community is preserved –
  there's a challenge to maintain and extend our work.

* Deuteronomy 15:12   † Charles Wesley

The best that any of us can be or become
is one of the 'friends of Jesus'.

He calls you to be his friend,
writes off all that you owe,
promises aid whenever you need it
– with no strings attached,
and gives us to each other – for ever.

Luke 16:19-31

RICH MAN, POOR MAN ⸻

This was a familiar 'rich man, poor man' story
   but Jesus gave it new meaning
   with a new beginning and a new end.

It is not about life beyond death;
   it does not tell the truth about heaven and hell;
   it is about the need on your doorstep.

The poor man

He was unattractive, diseased, disreputable;
   he had no power,
   no influential friends;
   he had nothing to give away;
   but he was called Lazarus!

Jesus, with his own view of people's value,
   added this deft touch;
   he gave the man a name.

The poor man is no longer simply poor;
   he is Lazarus!

He has a name.
He is a person,
   with his own individual worth,
   his own dignity and rights.

His name is Lazarus

Too weak to brush the dogs aside,
   he was so very vulnerable;
   and entirely dependent on other people.

He looked embarrassing;
   he was rejected and unwanted;
   but he was a man much-loved by God.

His name means 'God is my helper';

   and God helps those who cannot help themselves.

He helped Lazarus
   through those few who were prepared to carry him,
   and who had brought him to the rich man's gate.

The rich man

The rich man had no name,
   as if the only significant thing about him
   was that he was rich.

It's as if he had lost his identity in material things,
   lost his individuality in his many possessions;
   he was known simply as a rich man.

That's the great danger of materialism:
   people stop being people
   and simply become owners.

This man was independent and quite self-sufficient;
   he would not have got where he was
   if he had given to every beggar who got in his path.

Jesus looked hard at the scoffing Pharisees
   as he added his new ending.

This man had no time for the religion of his fathers;
   he certainly did not believe in miracles;
   he needed no help from God or anyone else.

He knew Lazarus was there on his doorstep;
   he knew his name and knew his need;
   and did nothing about it –

   that's the crux of the story.

On your doorstep
However you label them is irrelevant –
   alcoholic, drug-addict, prostitute, work-shy,
   foul-mouthed, vandal, scrounger, tramp –
   it's quite irrelevant:
   all that matters is their need.

If you know anyone in need
   you should tell your priest or minister;

   but that means you know too,
   and you can't just pass the buck.

Jesus said quite clearly
   if we possess the Scriptures
   and if we are not moved to action by human suffering
   nothing will change us.

Woe betide us if, knowing the need,
   we do nothing.

Any achievements in piety and religion fade away
   before that initial question:
   'I was hungry . . .'

Luke 17:5-10

TRUST AND OBEY _____

It hardly matters whether Jesus used
    a mulberry tree or a mountain *
    in his proverb-illustration;
    moving either would take some doing.

Faith
Faith can accomplish many things
    which at first may seem impossible.

Mind over matter can achieve much,
    faith over mind over matter even more.

Faith keeps on believing,
    even when experience seems to deny it;
    it keeps on hoping
    even when all previous hopes are shattered;
    it keeps on trusting God
    even when it seems he doesn't care;
    it keeps on loving till its last breath.

Lord, help me where faith falls short.

* Mark 11:22

Obedience

Religious belief may lead to wrong attitudes,
    proud and spiritually overbearing;
    true faith is never arrogant,
    nor exclusive, nor insensitive.

Pharisees thought they could put God in their debt
    by meritorious obedience;
    but faith is a gift, not an achievement.

Beware of any religion that seeks rewards;
    any good we may do is no more than we owe to God.

A servant who had worked hard all day
    could expect little or no thanks,
    it was only what he got paid for.

He may even have to do more;
    as we have learned from another parable *
    the reward for serving well
    is the opportunity for more service,
    and with greater responsibility.

Expect no special gratitude
    for doing what you are supposed to do;
    why should we expect God to be grateful to us
    when we have only done our duty anyway?

We have never done so superbly well
    that we deserve a break;
    there can be no retirement
    from serving Christ.

* Matthew 25:14

Until at that great banquet,
   which he is preparing for all people,
   by his pure, amazing grace,
   Christ will reverse the roles and wait on you;

   until then you are at his bidding
   to wait on him and serve him.

Faith must prove itself in action.

Luke 17:11-19

ONLY TEN PER CENT _____

If Jesus had known
  that nine would be so ungrateful,
  would he still have healed them?

Of course he would.

His help does not depend upon your gratitude
  or upon your faithfulness;
  all that matters is your need.

Whether or not you will be grateful,
  he will always give as much help
  as you will accept.

Separation
Luke emphasises separation:
  the border was a demarcation between Jew and Gentile,
  the Law required the lepers stood some way off
  and so they had to shout; *

Jesus also kept his distance
  and did not go to touch them
  as he had another leper.

* Leviticus 13

They were cleansed as they went on their way,
　　but the distance between them and Jesus was increasing.

Luke, himself a Gentile,
　　was eager to stress that one was a Samaritan.

Samaritans were hated and despised
　　and lepers were outcast from society;
　　this man was rejected on both counts;

　　but he had been accepted by this band of lepers.

In extremes of common need and desperation
　　old antagonisms and suspicions are often superseded,
　　previous fears dispelled by common cause.

When he knew his leprosy was healed,
　　this one came back to Jesus
　　and fell at his feet in gratitude and praise.

No social, racial, or religious divisions now;
　　not only acute privation can break down barriers,
　　so can Jesus, with his unconditional love.

The cleansed Samaritan came back
　　to the one who can heal diseases and divisions,
　　and found that Jesus can give not only physical healing
　　but forgiveness and wholeness,
　　reconciliation and eternal life.

Lasting gratitude
But what about the other nine?

Presumably, as orthodox Jews,
they had gone to the priests at the Temple
to make the appropriate sacrifices. *

* Leviticus 14

They too were praising God for their cleansing;
    but that was not enough for Jesus;
    he had so much more to give.

It is very natural, when we are in serious trouble,
    to cry out to God for help;

    and it is all too human,
    when the crisis passes
    or we have got what we wanted,
    to move further away from him than we were before.

These nine had come near to Christ;
    they knew his name and believed he could help;
    but they walked away from a greater gift
    than mere physical healing.

There is little point in berating them,
    or any we think are like them;
    but what about ourselves?

We all take so much for granted –
    countless daily blessings,
    our families and friends,
    and God.

We could spend more time in thanking God
    than in asking him for things.

Falling at his feet in praise,
    as did the healed Samaritan,
    we too may receive from Christ
    forgiveness and wholeness,
    healing and reconciliation,
    and eternal life.

Luke 18:1-8

DON'T LOSE HEART _____

We don't always recognise the humour of Jesus
   or spot his jokes.

There was a delighted chuckle
   when the magistrate in this story said:
   'If I don't do what this old woman wants,
   she'll give me a black eye!'

Most pleas for justice were taken to one of the elders
   but civil complaints were presented to a magistrate.

They were appointed by Herod or the Romans
   and were notoriously lazy and corrupt;
   to achieve any action or response
   they had to be bribed or threatened.

An impoverished widow,
   the epitome of defenceless, weak, exploited people,
   would stand little chance of any redress.

God is the very opposite of that magistrate.

He cares for people, especially for the poor,
   he does not have to be bribed or threatened
   or badgered into helping. *

* See page 212.

Don't give up

Luke kept meeting people
　　who had despaired of praying, and given up;
　　of all the Gospels, his is most concerned with prayer
　　and he wanted to encourage persistence.

They kept praying for the Kingdom,
　　but it did not come.

They prayed for justice and deliverance
　　but their prayers were not answered.

God seemed indifferent to their pleading.
Did he hear them?
Did he really care?
Why did he not intervene?

It was a familiar problem.

Faith and prayer

What you believe about prayer
　　depends on what you believe about God.

Of course he cares;
　　that's not the question.

In the light of Jesus, you know he cares;
　　but does he have favourites?
Should we expect preferential treatment?

Of course he hears;
　　that's not the problem.

The problem about hearing is his
　　– persuading us to listen to him.

God is not far off,
    waiting for our summons to intervene on our behalf;
    he is closer than breathing,
    nearer to us than hands and feet,
    patiently waiting for our response to him.

God is everywhere at work,
    willing only good for his creation,
    loving all his creatures,
    patiently longing, aching, to bring all to unity.

He will not force, or bribe, or threaten people,
    just as he himself will not be.

You can expect no more intervention
    than he has already made –
    on a Friday afternoon,
    on a hill outside a city wall,
    two thousand years ago.

You can, however, expect cooperation
    – if you will cooperate with him
    and share in what he is already doing.

The prayer of faith
    does not expect that God will give us all we ask
    – if only we trust him enough.

Faithful prayer
    joins our love to his constant loving,
    our wants to his eternal longing.

Prayer joins our eyes to the way he sees,
    and our minds and hearts, our hands and feet,
    as instruments of grace
    in what he is already doing.

The prayer of faith is faithful –
keeps on trusting him,
and keeps on praying.

Luke 18:9-14

PRAYER PATTERN _____

One day long ago,
    Isaiah went into the Temple in Jerusalem
    and saw a vision of God –
    his majesty and holiness and power;
    it seemed his presence filled the place.

Isaiah trembled in awe and wonder,
    aware of his own sinfulness,
    feeling most unworthy to be there.

Such is the beginning of worship and of prayer –
    praise and wonder for what God is,
    and penitence for what we are.

Penitence

Jesus told of a tax collector,
    in an inconspicuous corner of the Temple,
    standing at a distance like a leper,
    his head and shoulders bent.

He was not a good man:
    he had cheated and exploited people;
    he had neglected the Law;
    he fully deserved God's condemnation.

It had taken some courage
>for him to come into the Temple at all,
>and now he felt so out of place and so unworthy.

He was only aware of God's presence and of his own,
>and of the great gulf between them
>that he could not bridge.

He realised and admitted his faults
>and was truly penitent.

True worship needs humility like his –
>God can only establish real contact
>with a broken and contrite heart.

Arrogance

At the same time, in a more prominent place,
>standing upright, proud, and self-confident,
>was a Pharisee.

He was a good man,
>his devotion going beyond what the Law required.

Fasting was necessary only once a year
>but many Pharisees fasted twice a week:
>every Monday and Thursday,
>which just happened to be market days,
>they whitened their faces, wore ragged clothes
>and looked thoroughly miserable
>as they mingled with the crowds,
>parading their piety. *

A tithe was expected of all agricultural produce
>to sustain the Levite priests;

* See Matthew 6:16-18.

commendably Pharisees paid a tithe on everything
– and made sure that everybody knew.

He despised that tax-collector;
   it is all too easy to condemn
   those who do not conform to our (high) standards.

Other people are not the yardstick
   against which to measure ourselves –
   Christ is;
   and none of us measure up to him.

Listing his personal merit,
   the Pharisee did not realise
   how much he needed God's forgiveness.

He was so smug, self-satisfied and censorious,
   God could find no entrance past his pride.

Prayer pattern

The most-commended pattern, summarised A.C.T.S.,
   adoration, confession, thanksgiving and supplication –
   is the proper sequence for our prayers.

Only when we have affirmed God's presence
   (perhaps using a symbol such as a cross or candle)
   and bowed in adoration;

   only when we have frankly admitted our sin,
   our frailty and unloving;

   only when we have thanked him
   for his assured forgiveness,
   and for all he has done for us;

   only then can we relax in his Love
   and start asking.

Luke 6:20-31

In Luke's record of the 'Beatitudes' Jesus speaks only to his
disciples. It is shorter than Matthew's version; and Luke
alone records contrasting 'woes' where all the virtues are
reversed.

ALL THE SAINTS _____

Jesus spoke frankly to his disciples
   who would know poverty, hunger, and persecution
   for the sake of the Kingdom;

   his words had deep spiritual meaning
   but warned of the physical privation they were facing.

He encouraged them with the assurance
   that the felicity of the Kingdom was well worth it.

'O the good fortune of those who now can know
   what kings and prophets have longed to see.'

All Saints' Day
The gospel appointed to be read on this day
   is always a version of the Beatitudes;
   and I call to mind:

   Francis of Assisi, Ignatius Loyola, John Bunyan,
   and all whose poverty was both spiritual and economic;

all who have longed and worked for justice to prevail,
like Thomas More, John Wesley, Martin Luther King;

Mary of Magdala, William Blake, William Wilberforce,
and all who have shed tears for the tragedies of sin;

all who have suffered persecution for their faith,
like Peter, Paul, James, Thomas Becket, Catherine,
Joan, Alban, Lucy, Cranmer, Latimer, Ridley, Margaret;
and many, in more recent times, like Elizabeth Pilenko,
Maximilian Kolbe, Janani Luwum, Oscar Romero.

Today's reading prompts me to recall
Martin Neimoller, loving his enemies,
Boniface, doing good to those who hated him,
Dietrich Bonhoeffer, blessing those who cursed him,
Stephen, praying for those who treated him spitefully,
George Fox, preaching non-retaliation,
Barnabas and Matthew and their generosity.

My pulse quickens,
adrenalin flows freely,
and excitement mounts,
as more names come to mind:

Andrew, Mark, Bartholomew, Thomas,
Luke, Augustine, Aquinas, Abelard,
Patrick, Aidan, Columba, Cuthbert, Bede,
Hilda, Bernard, Theresa, Luther, Calvin,
Charles Wesley, Isaac Watts, John Henry Newman,
Booth, Schweitzer, Temple, and good Pope John;

and others whose names you want to add
who are especially precious to you.

Time is too short to tell of all we know,
but what a roll-call it would be!

Scholars, teachers, apostles, martyrs;
   some canonised, some not;
   some uncomfortable to live with,
   some most holy and a blessing to have met.

With Richard Baxter, I want to sing
   'In the communion of the saints
   is wisdom, safety, and delight'.

The holy mountain

I go, in heart and mind, to Transfiguration mountain
   where the glorified Christ had brought his friends,
   Simon, leader of the church, and later crucified,
   James, later beheaded for his faith,
   and John, evangelist, poet and theologian,
   and joined them with Moses and Elijah
   at the edge of space and time.

When we come in worship and in prayer,
   he brings us there too,
   to the edge of eternity,
   and joins us with those five
   and with all the company of heaven,
   with all who have gone before us.

Give praise to Christ,
   Lord of the Church and King of Saints,
   for all who have faithfully lived and died;

   and pray earnestly for the grace you need
   to follow Christ and them,
   and share that eternal joy.

For verses 20 to 26 see *Sunday by Sunday*, volume 1, page 77; for verses 27 to 31 see volume 1, page 79.

Luke 19:1-10

SMALL MAN, TALL ORDER _____

Greatness does not depend on size or stature;
    there have been many great and saintly men
    who were not very tall.

I have known others who were quite pompous,
    always wanting to impress,
    as if our significance is related to our height.

Many of us would like to think we are important,
    not only to ourselves and to God,
    not only to our families and friends,
    but in the world.

We are tempted to cultivate influential friends,
    or practise name-dropping,
    or try to say clever and surprising things,
    or criticise other people (but seldom to their faces),
    or gossip about them to show how informed we are
    and how superior we are to them:
    all such ploys are patently obvious and unloving.

Humility
Zacchaeus knew he had made his mark
    from all the wealth he had amassed,
    and from the cat calls that followed him in the street.

He'd had to learn to be quite thick-skinned
   to ignore the public slights and cries of 'Traitor!'

He was intrigued by what he had heard
   about the rabbi from Nazareth,
   and understood that Jesus had a tax collector
   amongst his closest friends.

Children laughed to see Zacchaeus running
   and jeered when he climbed the tree;

   but there was nothing else for it –
   he had to forget his dignity and assumed pomposity
   and hoist his robes and run and climb –
   he wanted so much to see Jesus for himself.

He was out of breath with climbing;
   it was much harder than he remembered;
   he'd always enjoyed climbing trees in his boyhood.

It was most exhilarating to see over the crowd
   and even more exciting to see Jesus.

When their eyes met,
   the encounter led to so much more
   than Zacchaeus had ever imagined.

Unless you become as a child again,
   unless you forget your pride and self-importance
   you will not see Jesus or the Kingdom.

Restitution

Wanting to put wrongs right,
   as far as you possibly can,
   is part of true repentance,
   though it is far easier said than done;

and we may never know
some of the harm that we have done.

An unkind action or thoughtless word
    may set up a chain reaction,
    with consequences far beyond our realisation,
    spreading out like ripples in a pool,
    adding to the web of evil in the world.

There is also a countering network of good,
    to which you may add and which you may strengthen
    by forgiveness and patience and love.

Zacchaeus giving half to charity, there and then,
    is quite a challenge to us, here and now.

Discipleship

Being a disciple of Jesus
    means becoming as a child,
    trying to see him more clearly,
    welcoming him into your home and heart,
    putting wrong things right
    and sharing generously with the poor.

Luke 20:27-38

THE LIVING GOD _____

After the scribes and Pharisees
   with their baited question about taxes,
   came the Sadducees.

The richest and most powerful men in the city,
   they were the ones behind the exploitation of pilgrims
   and the lucrative trading in the Gentiles' Court
   to which Jesus took a whip of cords.

Always mindful of their investments and their profit,
   they were resistant to any change
   and most conservative in attitude.

They recognised only the written law of Moses
   and were regularly at odds with Pharisees
   who were far more progressive in outlook,
   seeking to explore deeper applications of the faith,
   and wanting to extend its influence in the world.

These groups were renowned
   for their violent disagreement about resurrection.

There is the most appalling pun,
   which, once heard, will guarantee
   that you do not forget which was which:

Pharisees believed in resurrection
but Sadducees did not –
which was why they were so Sadd-u-cee!

They approached Jesus,
    wanting to ridicule any ideas of resurrection,
    just as today many will ridicule Christian belief.

Their silly story about levirate marriage
    gave Jesus opportunity to set the record straight.

Life beyond death

You must not think of heaven
    in earthly terms;
    it is so very different.

Heaven is far beyond what you can imagine –
    so it might be wiser not to try.

Many mansions and pearly gates
    are no more than first-century poetic attempts
    to describe the very best they could imagine,
    but heaven remains beyond human understanding.

I am more persuaded
    by the vision of G. A. Studdert-Kennedy
    (Woodbine Willie of the Flanders trenches) –
    no recording angel, no record books,
    no great white throne,
    but 'just him'.

Far better than anything we can imagine,
    I suspect we shall gasp with wonder
    at the simplicity and wonder of it;

    but all that I am sure of
    is that we shall be with Christ –
    and who need to know more?

The Living God

Jesus went further, to the delight of Pharisees,
    and spoke of the living God.

I am inspired and humbled by Abraham,
    father of three great monotheistic religions,
    a giant of faith who journeyed into the unknown,
    who had friendly talks with God,
    who worshipped as he travelled,
    who offered hospitality to strangers,
    who gave the better part to others,
    and who kept on trusting.

I learn a great deal from Isaac;
    but that God is the God of Jacob gives me hope.

Jacob was a cheat and a liar,
    and fled in fear of retribution.

But he learned that he could never run
    beyond the care and providence of God;
    he turned to this pursuing God and worshipped him.

He wrestled with God in the darkness
    to discover his true nature;
    and was given a new name and character;

    he repented and was reconciled to his brother,
    he fathered twelve sons and all the tribes of Israel.

The ground of our hope of heaven
    is in the living God
    who pursues the wanderer,
    forgives the penitent,
    and gives us a new name and character.

We shall never go beyond his love and care.

Luke 21:5-19

Luke was writing after the destruction of the temple in AD 70.
He used a different tradition from Mark and Matthew.

DESTROY THIS TEMPLE _____

The Temple figured much at the trial of Jesus,
    in evidence supporting the charge of blasphemy.

Ever since his first visit as a boy,
    Jesus had loved the Temple,
    the centre and symbol of Israel's faith;
    he loved its crowds and festivals.

He had wept over it,
    cleared its outer courts of abuse,
    confronted and challenged its leaders.

Herod's Temple

To ingratiate himself with the Jews,
    Herod the Great gave the Temple a make-over
    and made it the greatest in the world.

He constructed an immense base,
    four times the area of St Paul's Cathedral,
    held by fine stone blocks, each 40 ft x 12 ft.

With plates of gold on its roof and walls
    and all its great pillars of white marble,

it looked, from a distance,
   like a dazzling hill of white and gold.

The most magnificent votive gift was from Herod –
   a great golden vine, symbol of Israel;
   the bunches of grapes were six foot high.

This huge, awe-inspiring complex,
   looked, and was meant to look,
   as if it would stand for ever.

And Jesus said it would all be destroyed.

Jesus and the Temple

Jesus wept over Jerusalem and the Temple
   because they did not recognise
   God's moment when it came.

He took a whip to the markets
   because those meant to be light to all the nations
   had built a great monument to prejudice.

He challenged Sadducees and Pharisees
   because they perverted true holiness
   and thought that God belonged to them.

He could see there was a limit
   to the rebelliousness Romans would tolerate.

A new temple

Christ's new temple,
   established by his resurrection,
   is the Church, which is his Body.

Aware that we belong to him, not he to us,
   there must be no prejudice among us,

no denying of our calling by our deeds,
no narrow limits to true holiness,
no imagined boundaries to God's presence,
no diluting of his love

or we shall bring destruction on ourselves.

Luke 23:33-43

KING OF LOVE ────────────────

Pilate did not realise the full force of the inscription,
    for what he wrote still stands;
    a Roman who did not believe in Jesus
    testified to his kingship – in three languages!

He intended a deliberate gibe at the priests,
    a calculated insult to the Jewish people,
    whom he did not like at all,
    rubbing their noses in their subjection to Rome.

Infuriated by Pilate and hating Jesus,
    they taunted this unlikely king
    as he carried the cross-beam to the Place of Skulls.

Forgive them

As the soldiers hammered home the nails,
    Jesus gritted his teeth against the pain,
    and kept on praying, 'Father, forgive them'.

He died as he had taught and lived.

His first word from the cross
    rightly stressed forgiveness –
    the essential heart of his message,
    and our deepest need.

His forgiving word
    embraces not only the soldiers
    or those who barracked and harried him there,

    but all who had brought him to this suffering;
    and all of us whose sins are cluttered at his feet.

So often we don't know we're doing either,
    but at the foot of the cross,
    we too may hear what the soldiers heard,
    and know that he forgives us anything, everything.

This is a King
    who forgives his enemies,
    and even the deepest hurt.

He knew such forgiveness without limit is essential.

Only because God is a forgiving Father
    can we live in harmony with him;
    only by forgiving one another
    can there be peace in any family,
    in a community, or in the world.

Alongside us

That Friday afternoon
    he was where you will always find him:
    with the outcasts,
    alongside those suffering and dying.

He hung there, totally exposed,
    entirely vulnerable to the taunts and ribaldry;
    while his enemies still gave vent to their hatred,
    and were still asking for a sign.

While the others scoffed and laughed at him,
only one man, a dying man, recognised the truth.

That condemned man, facing death,
    had no illusions about either himself or his fate
    and turned to Jesus;

    and Jesus, of course, was there for him,
    alongside him with compassion,
    with promise, and unexpected hope –
    'Take the next step with me'.

King of Love

This is an unexpected kind of King,
    who rides on a donkey,
    who washes his friends' feet,
    who turns a circle of thorns into a crown.

He forgives his enemies,
    he gives hope to a dying man,
    he makes a criminal's cross into a throne
    by which to draw all people to himself.

Today,
    if you will turn to him,
    and admit the truth about yourself –

    he will forgive you too
    and offer you new hope and a new beginning.

Alongside you now,
    alongside you at your end of days;

    forgiving you now,
    forgiving you then.

This is the amazing King of Love.

GOSPEL INDEX